MY ANCESTORS WERE THAMES WATERMEN

A GUIDE TO TRACING YOUR THAMES WATERMEN AND LIGHTERMEN ANCESTORS

by James W Legon

SOCIETY OF GENEALOGISTS ENTERPRISES LTD

Published by
Society of Genealogists Enterprises Limited
14 Charterhouse Buildings
Goswell Road
London EC1M 7BA

First edition 2006
Second edition 2008

© James W Legon 2008

ISBN 10: 1 903462 95 9
ISBN 13: 978 1 903462 95 9

British Library Cataloguing in Publication Data.
A CIP Catalogue record for this book is available from the British Library.

The Society of Genealogists Enterprises Limited is a wholly owned
subsidiary of the Society of Genealogists, a registered charity, no 233701.

About the Author

James W Legon is a descendant of eight generations of Thames Watermen
and Lightermen. He has transcribed numerous documents from the archives and his
enthusiasm for the subject is mirrored in his website at www.ParishRegister.com. He
runs a thriving family history and guided tour business, Docklands Ancestors Ltd.

James believes passionately in the need to preserve and disseminate the cultural history of
the Thames and its bygone occupations.

Cover Image - Charles Thomas Bullman, Doggett's Coat and Badge winner in 1876.
Picture courtesy of C. T. Bullman's great grand daughter, Sandra Jillings. Also shows
the badge that belonged to John Crawford of Rotherhithe and Retirement Cottages at
Penge, 1899 (background).

CONTENTS

LIST OF ILLUSTRATIONS

All other illustrations by kind permission of the Company of Watermen and Lightermen of the River Thames.

FOREWORD BY ROBERT J COTTRELL

Old Father Thames, that great meandering highway, dividing London and its suburbs, but always attracting an ever increasing population, like a flock of seagulls around a piece of bread. The River Thames, which ebbs and flows past those historic monuments and landmarks in London that we take for granted ; London's River.

For centuries the river has rewarded those who know its secrets, who tame it's eddies and recognise its dangers. The Thames watermen and lightermen is that special breed of workforce who respect what the river has to offer, who have learnt its secrets and are never too proud to admit that they have nothing new to learn. However, don't be fooled into thinking that the Thames watermen and lightermen are a romantic breed, stripped to the waist navigating their craft along its tidal length; you only have to check out the complaints book to understand that they have been the most vulgar, rough, foul-mouthed and dishonest band of characters you could ever have the privilege to rub shoulders with. Acts of parliament were forced upon them to regulate the craft, men and fares. The Company being a city guild never protected the majority of its workforce from the attractions of the press gangs, unlike the protected men belonging to the livery companies. It organised a strict training and apprenticeship system, constantly being updated to meet the demands of the time. In 1908 most of its powers passed to the Port of London Authority, although the Company still oversees its charities and almshouses. What the future holds is uncertain, times are still changing and perhaps the trade of watermen or lightermen will fade with the introduction of a National Boatmasters or Freight masters licence, a step towards a European licence, where we are all supposed to be equal.

When I started my labour of love, indexing the apprentice or binding records of the Company of Watermen & Lightermen, I was surprised that what I took for granted others did not. The expression "waterman" and "lighterman" was not clear to all, nor what they did, how they did it and what records existed. There seemed little understanding of the apprenticeship system, the information held within the binding books whereby you had to be over fourteen and under twenty to be bound to a freeman, and be able to prove it with the proof being entered within the affidavit books. Don't be sidetracked by entries in the census showing the occupation of a waterman as a pilot, or a lightermen as a tug captain; many watermen became legal dock, creek or local pilots. With the introduction of the tug our lightermen ancestors evolved into becoming tug captains or mates. The records that have survived are astounding and I trust James Legon's guide will gently point you in the right direction to solve the mystery of life and work on the River Thames for the watermen and lightermen.

Happy reading.
Rob Cottrell

ACKNOWLEDGMENTS

I am indebted first and foremost, to my friend and colleague, Robert J. Cottrell, for helping me to discover the fascinating world of the Thames Watermen and Lightermen.

Thanks too to Simon Burley and Eileen Richardson for their help and suggestions in writing this Guide.

I would also like to thank Colin Middlemiss, the present clerk to the Company, for responding to my numerous queries and for kindly giving permission to reproduce archive material and the Company Coat of Arms.

This work would not have been possible without the diligence of a previous clerk, Henry Humpherus, whose dedication in compiling History of the Origin and Progress of the Company of Watermen and Lightermen of the River Thames has been of such great help both to me and all other researchers into the history of this historic Company.

I would also like to thank Robert G. Crouch, a former Master of the Company, Queen's Royal Bargemaster and Doggett's Coat and Badge winner.

This Guide is dedicated to the memory of my grandfather, James William Legon 1895 –1969, last of the 8 generations of Legon Watermen and Lightermen.

1. "At Commandment of our Superiors"
Motto of the Company of Watermen & Lightermen

CHAPTER 1

WATERMEN AND LIGHTERMEN HISTORY

A Brief History of the Company

The Corporation of London was appointed Conservator of the Thames as long ago as 1193. Amongst its duties was the licensing of those operating boats on the river. The activities of watermen, those who carried people by boat, were further regulated by the Corporation in 1370.

Watermen's activities were regulated by Acts of Parliament in 1514 and 1555. These Acts covered the regulation of charges and boat safety. One can imagine the situation on the Thames at the time as similar to the activities of unlicensed minicab drivers of today. Complaints of over-charging and foul language were rife.

The Company of Watermen was brought into being in 1566 by Act of Parliament to further regulate the activities of Watermen. The Company differed from the other City livery companies in a very important way. It was set up not merely to protect the commercial interests of its members, but to regulate them as well. It remains the only Company to have been brought into being by such Act.

Its first coat of arms was granted by Elizabeth I in 1585 and its charter in 1827. The Coat depicts a shield, showing a rowing boat on water, below crossed oars and tasselled cushions, which represent the watermen's work carrying passengers on the river. The shield is supported by two dolphins and surmounted by a crest of a raised right arm holding a golden oar. "At commaundement of owre superiors" surmounts, the Company's motto.

The jurisdiction of the Company was from Gravesend in the east to Windsor in the west. This was shortened by the Thames Conservancy Act of 1857, to Teddington Lock in the west.

In 1696 the system of plying for trade at a designated place and the numbering of boats and operators was introduced. Tables of fares were an annual publication by the beginning of the 18th century. Appendix XI details the fares in use in 1671, which were previously increased in 1559.

The year 1700 saw the amalgamation of the lightermen into the Company, who previously had been members of the Woodmongers Company. The term lightermen refers to the process of lightening a ship of its load. The goods were then either rowed to shore, or loaded onto another ship.

2. Two examples of Thames lighters

The 18th century marked the beginning of the construction of London's bridges. The first was Blackfriars, finished in 1769. This led to a gradual decline in the need for watermen. By contrast, as the Port of London flourished the number of lightermen increased.

In the era before the building of the bridges, estimates vary about the number of watermen employed on the river. In the reign of Queen Elizabeth I there were estimated to be 3,000-4,000 working watermen (Taylor: The True Cause p6). An Admiralty census of 1629 recorded a figure of 2,426 (Public Record Office, SP 16/135, piece 4, see appendix XVI). A list of members from 1809 showing who they were working for is also to be found in Appendix XIII.

Governance of the Company was at first by its Rulers and Overseers, eight in number and from 1827 by a Master and Wardens. Mr Francis Theodore Hay was the first such Master of the Company. A full listing of Masters of the Company is to be found in Appendix I.

Masters and Apprentices

By 1555 if you wanted to work on the Thames on a boat, you had to be a member of the Company. To gain the Freedom of the Company you had to have served an apprenticeship. A badge had to be worn at all times, failure to do so resulted in a fine.

The usual age for an apprentice to start his apprenticeship was fourteen. Initially this was for one year, it was then increased to a period of seven years in 1603. In the 20th century it was shortened to five years. In many cases the apprentice was bound, (apprenticed) to his father. If the father died during the apprenticeship period it was not unusual for the mother to be named in his place.

The apprentice was not formally allowed to marry before completing his apprenticeship, (although plenty of examples can be found where they did marry).

3. *The badge that belonged to John Crawford of Rotherhithe who was bound 1st October 1789 and made free 20th October 1796.*

The masters' responsibility was both to teach the skills necessary for a life on the river and to provide board and lodging to his apprentice. Crucially, it should be noted that the operative phrase is actually cause to be taught, which explains the apprenticing of boys to their mothers, or other females, who clearly did not work on the river.

At the end of the apprenticeship period, master and apprentice presented themselves to the Company at Waterman's Hall at St Mary-At-Hill for examination, before gaining the Freedom of the Company.

The beginning of the apprenticeship was recorded in the archives of the Company. The apprentice's name was noted, the name of his master, his home parish and the date that the apprenticeship started. Later, the date that 'freedom' was gained was also added. This document is known as the 'apprenticeship binding'. It is these records that are the cornerstone for research into waterman ancestors.

The Company continues in existence to this day .Although trade on the river has much diminished, due, amongst many other reasons, to the deep water facilities available at Tilbury, Felixstowe and Harwich, the Company continues to apprentice people to a life on the River. You are most likely to meet a waterman if you take one of the popular river cruises, or espy a tug towing London's rubbish downstream.

4. The tug Mersina, St Paul's in the background, underway towing two rubbish lighters

Sadly, the end is now in sight for the licensing of watermen by the Company and the Port of London Authority. The Maritime and Coastguard Agency will be issuing National Boatmaster's Licences in 2007. Yet another piece of the rich tapestry of our heritage is to be done away with and centuries of tradition, pride and service swept away...

This guide is not intended to be a complete history of the Company. For that I strongly suggest the works of Henry Humpherus and Christopher O'Riordan, details of which can be found in the bibliography.

For contemporary accounts of lives spent working on the river Thames there are three books you should read. Ernest G. Murray's *Tales of a Thames Lighterman* contains a wonderful account of taking a barge under oars the length of the river. A longer account is to be found in the book by Dick Fagan and Eric Burgess, Men of the Tideway. Dick came from a family of lightermen who had worked the river for centuries. His words, published in 1966, recall the history, as well as the reality, of a life of hard graft on the Thames. The third is by Harry Harris, *Under Oars: Reminiscences of a Thames Lighterman, 1894-1909.*

Working Life of a Thames Lighterman

Most of our knowledge of the working life of a typical Thames lighterman comes from 20th century accounts, particularly from the writings of Ernest Murray, Harry Harris and Dick Fagan. They wrote from the perspective of being Thames lightermen at the busiest time for the trade, the middle of the 20th century.

From reading their accounts, it can be seen that the life was one of unremitting hard graft. A twenty hour day was not uncommon. The wages were poor and unemployment was rife. Getting work at all was at the whim of the labour master and men were fired out of hand on the flimsiest of pretexts. The work was often at night and in all kinds of weather. Many a lighterman would spend nights marooned afloat in a great London fog, praying his food, drink and fuel for his stove would last out. Many an apprentice suffered stories of the cannibal freemen who'd carved up the cabin boy during a great 'soup'!

Even in the days of steam tugs, capable of towing many barges, it was still cheaper to have lightermen row the cargo by hand. An apprentice's blisters were legendary. As was the parsimony of the lighterage companies, as they never had enough oars for all the boats. This 'encouraged' the lighterman to use his 'enterprise' to solve the problem.

Pilfering was rife, but times were hard. The trick was obviously not to get caught and elaborate lengths were gone to. Large pockets sewn inside a jacket, riverside safe houses and the corruption of officials were commonplace. The large walls enclosing the docks were to keep the public out, and the goods in. Police were employed at the dock gates and the river had its own dedicated River Police. As fellow Thames workers, even the lightermen never had a bad word to say about them.

The lightermen considered themselves the aristocrats of the Thames. This was for several reasons. As skilled men who had served an apprenticeship they naturally considered themselves better than the motley crew employed as dockers. This was reflected not only in their wages, (higher than a docker's, or stevedore's), but in their dress as well.

In the early 20th century the accepted attire consisted of a navy blue serge suit, waterproof thick soled boots, a stiff white collar and a bowler hat. This was topped off with a watch on a chain (a 'slang') stretched across the waistcoat and kept in the right hand pocket. In winter this outfit was completed by a thick Melton coat, with a velvet collar, (considered de rigueur).

5. *Lighterman's 'slang' that belonged to J. W. Legon*

(The first possession of my grandfather's that came my way was just such a watch. It was to be over thirty years before I discovered its significance).

A typical day in the working life of a lighterman would begin the previous afternoon with a telephone call to his firm's offices to get his instructions. The labour master would tell the lighterman where to be, at what time, and what the task was. "Limehouse Cut, six o'clock, *Cadet* to Aberdeen" for example. Limehouse Cut being the place, Cadet being the name of the barge and Aberdeen meaning Aberdeen Wharf, also in Limehouse.

A six o'clock start meant exactly that. As the saying goes "time and tide wait for no man". The Thames is tidal, meaning that if you missed the tide your boat was not going anywhere.

Having arrived after possibly a train and/or bus journey, or more likely a foot slog, it was then a matter of identifying the boat and casting off. This usually meant hauling in an icy, wet, mud-clammy five inch rope.

Once out on the river, the lighterman would use his knowledge of the tides and river geography to navigate his way to his destination. This might be to another ship to load/unload cargo, to a dock or wharf to load/unload. Laden with up to fifty tons of cargo, and using nothing more than a large pair of oars, the lighterman was responsible for the safe arrival of cargo and boat.

This often meant 'shooting the bridges', where the current was at its strongest. Even the best of swimmers stood no chance if they fell in, such was the strength of the current. A common fate for many a lighterman was a watery grave, (and not always alcohol related!).

The lighterman was not responsible for actually loading the boat. That was done by stevedores or dockers. What he did have to do was tally the cargo and ensure it was safely stowed. He would then cover it up with tarpaulins and secure it with rope.

The cargo could be just about anything: Timber, barrels of rum, meat, bales of wool, chemicals, sugar, fruit, ivory, spices, tobacco to name but a few.

6. The last of the Thames Paddle Steamers, Waverley, under tow at Tower Pier

Employment Status of Watermen and Lightermen

I am frequently asked whether watermen and lightermen were employed or self employed, and a great deal of confusion surrounds the subject. Looking first at watermen, we are dealing with matters that stretched backwards in time from their heyday in the 17th century. The primary source material is pretty much silent on the subject. Appendix XIII, from Humpherus, lists the avocation, or employment status of some 5,000 watermen in 1809. It can be seen that most were in the employ of some body or other, the commissioners of the Navy and Admiralty for example. Nearly 20% were employed in the Navy itself. It would be fair to assume then that at this time, most watermen could be categorised as employed.

Further back in time, the picture is not as clear. In 1628 however, the Admiralty Muster of 1628/29 shows that nearly half the men had made at least one sea voyage, showing that the Navy was even then a major 'source of employment', (if one can put it that way, as they probably had no choice in the matter).

The various bodies that were employing men in 1809 were for the most part in existence then too, and would have been employers of watermen. However, there were far more watermen in the earlier days, before roads and bridges came along. It is this body of men that were far more likely to have been self employed. Indeed it is from them, and this period, that the popular, or romantic, picture of the jolly (abusive) waterman derives from. The books and pamphlets of John Stow and the diaries of Samuel Pepys make plain that the Thames was awash with individual watermen competing and touting for business. Further evidence can be seen in the City of London's Collage collection of paintings.

The employment status of lightermen is probably clearer, as they came into history far later, with their heyday being in the 20th century. Which is not to say that there have not always been lightermen. Indeed, in January 1642, the House of Lords considered an "An Act to restrain bargemen, lightermen and others from labouring and working on the Lord's day, commonly called Sunday." (HL/PO/JO/10/2/8).

The lighterage trade probably came into existence the moment a ship was too large to moor alongside a jetty, or jetty and wharf space became too crowded. But in the centuries after their amalgamation with the watermen in 1700, it would probably be fair to say that most lightermen were in the employ of a lighterage firm. Appendix VII lists a small portion of these.

The Great Dock Age

As we have seen, the building of bridges over the Thames, together with the arrival of horse drawn transport on roads, paved the way for the gradual decline in the numbers of watermen. This coincided with the rise of the British Empire, centred as it was on London, and in particular on the Thames. In every century until the late 20th century, London was the biggest port in the country. A major reason why this was so was the passing of the Navigation Acts. The first of these, passed in 1381, but more particularly the Acts of 1650, 1660 and 1663, forbade foreign ships to trade in British colonies, forbade the importation of goods except in English vessels or in vessels of the country of origin of the goods, (which lead to the Anglo-Dutch War of 1652-54), and required that all colonial products could only be exported in British ships. This lead to an explosion in the shipping trade of this country, with London the only port remotely capable of handling the vast amounts of cargo.

The Thames, being obviously limited in both its size and depth, quickly ran out of space to handle the vast numbers of ships wishing to load or unload. This lead to the building of London's docks, beginning with the West India Docks in 1802. With the completion of the Royal Group in 1921, (Victoria, Albert and King George V), London had more water enclosed in docks than anywhere else, before or since. (Please refer to Appendix

VI for a brief timeline of the Thames and to Appendix XIV for a brief history of London's docks).

This at first brought great consternation to the lightermen, who prior to the building of the docks, thrived on unloading cargo 'over the side' in the Thames. Indeed, vested interests delayed the passing of the West India Docks Act by five years. However, a clause in the 1799 Act gave wharf owners and lightermen the right to send craft into the docks to collect goods for the riverside wharves and to deliver exports to ships in the dock without incurring any charges.

This became known as the 'free water clause' and it was kept in all successive legislation relating to dock building. The 'free water clause' was to effect greatly the operating of the port during the following years and proved to be the salvation of the lightermen.

The demise of the docks, from the 1960s to the 1980s, has been written about, argued over bitterly and been the source of much strife. What is beyond dispute is that as ship sizes increased beyond the capacity of the Thames to handle them, new deep water facilities were needed. Containerisation also played a part in the demise of the docks. Today, the deep water facilities of Felixstowe and Harwich account for much of the import and export trade of the UK.

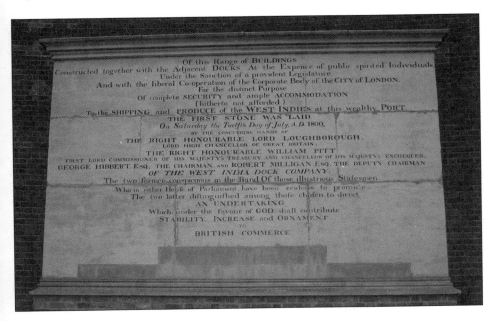

7. Memorial stone at the entrance to the West India Docks

Doggett's Coat and Badge Race

The oldest annual sporting event in the world is rowed each year between London Bridge and the Swan, Chelsea, a furlong short of five miles. Named after Thomas Doggett, an Irish actor and comedian, it was inaugurated in 1715 with the prize of a scarlet coat and a silver badge. The race is contested by six Watermen within a year of the completion of their apprenticeship.

Doggett, a Whig, was described as a political comedian and commented on Parliament. He was pleased at the accession of the new Hanoverian King, George I and the race was his way of commemorating the event. It is held on 1st August each year.

Sponsoring a race was a common event of the times, but Doggett's Coat & Badge Wager is the only one that survives. As the executors of his will, the Fishmongers' Company ensured the event survived his death in 1721 and continues to this day.

The boats used initially in the race were four-seater passenger wherries; banana shaped with shallow draughts able to ground for the loading and off-loading of passengers. These were rowed by one man, using two oars. Beadles were appointed to ensure against the practice of 'tickling', whereby the boat was lightened by sanding down the planks.

Until 1873 the race was rowed against the tide and thereafter with the tide.

Doggett's Will stipulated the cost of the Coat and Badge- "Five pounds for a Badge of Silver weighing about 12 ounces and representing Liberty to be given to be rowed for by Six young Watermen according to my Custom, Eighteen Shillings for Cloth for a livery whereon the said Badge is to be put, one pound one shilling for making up the said Livery and Buttons and Appertunances to it."

The race is still held to this day and a list of winners is detailed in Appendix II. Many people have been told as part of family legends that they have an ancestor who won Doggett's and the list of winners is often their starting point to family history research.

8. Charles Thomas Bullman, Doggett's Coat and Badge winner in 1876.
Picture courtesy of C. T. Bullman's great grand daughter, Sandra Jillings.

Watermen and the Monarchy

Watermen have been associated with the monarchy from the very beginning, an association that continues to this day. The reason for this association lies in the very foundations of the City of London being adjacent to the Thames. As soon as monarchs established their presence in the capital they have used river transport as their preferred means of transport. This was because roads as we know them did not exist and a sumptuously kitted out barge was far more comfortable than a horse drawn carriage.

The system of royalty having dedicated barges and Royal Watermen coincided too with the building of London's great royal palaces. A glance at any map of London quickly reveals that the majority of these were situated on the banks of the Thames. Beginning with the Palace of Westminster, royal residences were to be found at the Tower of London, Whitehall, Greenwich, Hampton Court, Windsor, Kew, as well as at Buckingham, St James's and Kensington Palaces. When one considers the sewage arrangements prevalent in London until quite recently, that is, chuck it out the window into the street, it takes no great leap of imagination to understand why royalty took the water road.

The Civil War period highlights the link between watermen and monarchy. The City of London was by and large pro Parliament, but the watermen went against this grain and was open in its support for the King. This is amply demonstrated by a petition of 1648, (House of Lords, HL/PO/JO/10/2/11):

"To the Right Honourable the Lords assembled in Parliament. The humble petition of the watermen belonging to the River of Thames. Shews, that these petitioners being in family above twenty thousand persons, are all undone, and like to perish, by reason of his Majesty's absence from us, being kept away notwithstanding his many former gracious offers, and therefore having an interest both in his person and government, we cannot do less than humbly beseech your honours speedily and really to invite him to London with honour, freedom & safety. And ye petitioners shall praie."

The petition lists the names of 2,026 watermen, (although some names are duplicated). I hesitate to say it was signed by these men, as it was actually written by one man, the clerk to the Company, Thomas Lowe. Various estimates put the total number of watermen at the time at around 2,500 – 4,000. Thus, it can be seen that the petition does probably reflect the majority opinion amongst the watermen.

The petition was organised by Nowell Warner, the King's Royal Bargemaster, and Robert Burssey. The Warner family, of Greenwich, had long been associated with royalty. Richard Warner the elder had been Bargemaster to Queen Elizabeth and subsequently to James I's queen until both she and Warner died in 1612. Richard the younger was Bargemaster to James I. His son, Nowell Warner, had been appointed junior Bargemaster in 1614 to replace Richard the elder. He then became senior Bargemaster to Charles I.

Following the King's execution in 1649, the Royal Watermen were dismissed, although a few were kept on in the service of the Commonwealth. The Restoration in 1660 saw the reinstatement of the Royal Watermen. Nowell Warner's son John became Bargemaster to Charles II, and subsequently to William III.
In 1641 there were forty-four watermen serving the King and lesser numbers of Queen's and Prince's watermen. The Royal Bargemasters were in charge. Two King's Bargemasters were appointed jointly, with the 'junior' of these, when there was a Queen, the Queen's Bargemaster.
The Bargemasters were paid an annual 'retainer', £30 for example in the seventeenth century to the King's Bargemaster. The watermen's income was, however, earned for specific services. Invoices can be found in the National Archives showing their requests for payment for various services rendered. Thus it can be seen that loyalty to royalty was, in part at least, in the watermen's financial self interest.

The appointment of Royal Watermen and Queen's Bargemasters continues to this day, their numbers being maintained at twenty two. Their most important ceremonial duties are the transportation of the Crown Jewels, by river, from the Tower to Westminster for the Coronation, although no longer performing the duty of rowing the monarch.
The Crown and State Regalia are delivered to the Palace of Westminster at the State Opening of Parliament by the Royal Watermen.

To become a Royal Waterman a licensed Thames Watermen has to apply to the Lord Chamberlain. Their number is always maintained at 22. After sometimes waiting for many years, they are interviewed at Buckingham Palace and if successful, appointed to a short list to replace retiring Royal Watermen.

Waterman's Hall

The first hall of the Company was reputed to be Coldharbour Mansion, just upstream of London Bridge. In History and Progress of the Company of Watermen & Lightermen, Henry Humpherus certainly believed this to be the case. I however am persuaded by Christopher O'Riordan in The Thames Watermen in the Century of Revolution that this was not the case.

The first hall was in fact situated at Three Cranes Wharf, south of the Guildhall, in Broad Lane. It was leased from the Merchants Taylors' Company in 1565, for an annual lease of £66 and a rent of £8, the lease being renewable at 21 year intervals.

This hall was burnt down in the Great Fire of 1666 and a new hall built on the site of Coldharbour Mansion. This second hall continued in use until it was rebuilt on the same site in 1721

The present, 4th hall, was built in 1780 and can be seen today situated in St Mary At Hill, close by the Thames. It was designed by William Blackburn, who is also noted as being the leading designer of prisons of his time. Built in the classical style, with Croade stone decoration, the hall remains the only original Georgian Hall left in the City of London.

The hall was damaged by bombing in the War and repairs were not completed until 1951. It was extended in 1983 to include bigger dining and meeting facilities, with the acquisition of two adjacent buildings, including the former Fellowship Porters Hall. An anteroom on the ground floor is panelled with timber from demolished riverside warehouses.

All Watermen and Lightermen have passed through the hallowed doors to be examined by the Court at the time of their Binding and Freedom admission.

9. The Master's chair at Waterman's Hall

10. Waterman's Hall

Watermen and the Navy

For many hundreds of years both the monarchy and later the Royal Navy found the watermen of the Thames a ready source for manning the Navy. As far back as 1337, King Edward III, when pursuing his claim to the throne of France, manned his fleet using men from the Thames. The practice undoubtedly stretches back to the dawn of history in these isles. Any king, with his capital in London, presented with a shortage of manpower, would have found it irresistible not to have drawn upon the water based workforce on his very doorstep.

The 1628 Admiralty survey of nearly 2,400 watermen, records that nearly half the men had served at sea. (One indeed, the 56 year old John Warden of Rederife, had amassed a total of 100 voyages).

The Revolutionary and Napoleonic wars of the 18th and early 19th centuries saw the practice of impressing men into the Navy at its height. The popular image of a gang of toughs waylaying the hapless victim, whilst having its basis in fact, disguises the systematic and organised way in which the practice applied to the watermen of the Thames. It was far more expedient simply to require the Company to produce the required number of men.

In the century to 1800, Humpherus records in *History & Origin* approximately 70 occasions when the Admiralty issued orders for the impressment of watermen. Disputes were frequent, as to who exactly could be pressed and who was 'protected' from the press. In theory apprentices were protected, as were holders of passes, issued usually to the watermen of important people, such as the Lord Mayor's watermen. These passes, which contain a physical description of the holder, are of enormous interest for those with waterman ancestors. In particularly severe emergencies, such as in 1776 during the American War of Independence, a 'hot' press was issued, when all such protections were cancelled. On the 28th October warrants were issued by the Admiralty and eight hundred men were taken, leaving none but masters, mates and boys.

Impressment explains why so many apprentices did not complete their apprenticeship, or took many more years than usual to do so, throughout this period. Appendix IX lists the names of 105 watermen who were killed in action or invalided from the service in the period 1803-09.

Impressment was only formally brought to an end with the introduction in 1853 of continual service for sailors. *Enter the Press-Gang*, by Daniel James Ellis, gives a fascinating insight into the impact of impressment in contemporary literature, examining the case both for and against what would nowadays be termed slavery.

Almshouses and Charities

Concern for watermen too old to work pre-dates concern in society at large for what we now term pensioners, by centuries. Henry VI for example, erected almshouses, known as St Stephens, at Westminster in 1442. In 1742, Captain John Fell, a Ruler of the Company, bequeathed in his will four almshouses at Blackwall, for the 'poor watermen of Blackwall'. In 1824 a report was delivered from the Charity Commissioners concerning the very same almshouse erected by Henry VI ! Henry Humpherus notes that in 1826 the almshouses at Woolwich 'endowed by Sir Martin Bowes, Knight, who was Lord Mayor of London in the year 1545, and were rebuilt by the Company of Goldsmith's, London, in the year 1771' were not now inhabited by freemen of the Company.

It was in 1808 that the Company first concerned itself with the provision of almshouses for its retired members, with a subscription being opened for an 'asylum for the poor of the Company'. Nothing much seems to have become of this, the matter being raised again in 1812. It was not until 1838 that a committee was appointed to look seriously at the matter. (Appendix XV lists the amounts donated by the Court of the Company).

It was the gift by Mr John Dudin Brown of two acres, (later increased), of land at Penge and the donation of £200 by Mr Alderman Lucas that really got the ball rolling. The appointment of the Dowager Queen Adelaide as patroness of the project, (and her donation of £100) added further impetus and in 1839 a contract was entered into for the erection of 30 almshouses at Penge. These cottages remained in use until 1973, when the inhabitants were transferred to new bungalows at Hastings. The buildings were then used for public, and subsequently private housing.

11. Retirement Cottages at Penge, 1899

A further charity, the Home Cottages, was established in 1881 at Ditchling by Mr William Vokins, a Master Lighterman of the prominent lighterage company, Vokins & Co. Both of these charities were reorganised in 2000 into the Royal Cottage Homes for Watermen.

The Company maintains its charities to this day. The Benevolent Fund of The Company was formed in July 2000 following the reconstruction of the charities of The Company of Watermen and Lightermen. The charity, formerly the General Benevolent Fund was founded by the Company by Declaration of Trust in 1930. The Fund raises money for the benefit of one of the connecting charities, the Royal Cottage Homes for Watermen, which has almshouses in Hastings and Ditchling. It also raises money to give grants to needy Freemen of The Company.

The Philip Henman Foundation was founded by deed in 1961 with a gift from Dr Henman of shares of the Transport Development Group worth £10,000. The income was used to promote and encourage post school education and training for persons engaged in the port transport industry. The principal object of the trust continues to be the education of young people making or intending to make a career on or in connection with the River Thames. The objects of the Charity were expanded to enable fund-raising and further activities to take place.

12. Annual outing of the lightermen of Wrightson & Sons 1925

CHAPTER 2

TRACING YOUR WATERMEN AND LIGHTERMEN ANCESTORS

This chapter deals with the various sources available to the family historian to research. It is written from the perspective that not everyone will be able to personally visit the various repositories for themselves. Copious reference is therefore made to the various sources that can be found on the internet. I would stress right from the start however that the information that you find on the Internet cannot be regarded as conclusive evidence. Best practice is to always verify the information at the original source and to seek supporting evidence.

Addresses and contact details for all the sources mentioned are provided at the end of this guide in Appendix V

Family historians researching ancestors identified as Watermen or Lightermen can count themselves truly blessed! A wealth of material survives, dating back to at least 1629. The trade of Watermen or Lightermen was in many, many cases passed down from father to son. This enables the family historian to reach back over many generations for vital information on the family's history.

I will now outline the main avenues of research open to the family historian for researching watermen and lightermen ancestors, beginning with the most important.

The Manuscripts Section, Guildhall Library

The Great Fire of London in 1666 destroyed nearly all of the Company's records, with only three items saved from the flames. All the surviving records of the Company from 1688 to the early 20th century, are housed at The Guildhall, Aldermanbury, London and many have been microfilmed. Records after this date remain at Waterman's Hall.

The Corporation of London Record Office houses the order books and papers of the Court of Aldermen from the 17th century and these provide much detail on the history of the Company.

In the same building, the manuscript section of the Guildhall Library is where the majority of the Company's archives are to be found. You do not need to book a visit and there is no charge to view the material. As with all record offices only pencils are allowed. Appendix X lists in full the material held.

The most useful of these records for the family historian are the Apprenticeship Bindings Indexes, (MS6289). This is the best place to start your research.

The microfilmed originals have been transcribed and indexed by Robert J Cottrell and cover the period 1692 to 1949. This was a 4 year project and a monumental achievement by one of the UK's leading transcribers.

The result of his work is that, either at the Guildhall Library, or from home, you can search these records, which are indexed alphabetically. If you are able to visit the Guildhall in person, begin with the indexes on microfiche and note the details of each instance of the name you are researching.

Next, go to the microfilms, housed in the large grey metal cabinets, covering the periods you have noted from the microfiche. You can then easily find the entry and obtain a print out.

It should be stressed that indexes and transcriptions should always be checked against the original record. Whilst these indexes are extremely useful to the family historian it is important to realise that transcription is an art, not a science. Mention must also be made here of the necessity of keeping accurate records of what you have searched.

The information recorded in the Bindings Indexes is as follows:

Name of the apprentice; surname followed by forenames
Date of Binding
Location
Name of Master or Mistress
Date of Freedom, if granted. The completion of the apprenticeship).

13. Apprenticeship Binding of John Leghorne 1717
MS6289 Guildhall Library

As mentioned previously, the usual period of apprenticeship was seven years. It is not uncommon however to find much longer periods recorded. Thomas Legon, for example, was bound in 1785 but did not complete his apprenticeship until 1796. A common reason for this was impressment into the navy. This was probably the case with Thomas Legon, as later research found that he was discharged, wounded, from HMS Achille in 1802 (MS6386)

You will also find many examples of apprenticeships not completed at all. This could be for many reasons, impressment again being one of these. Appendix XII gives a partial listing of the numbers of apprentices bound each year, together with the subsequent number of freedoms granted.

If you are not able to visit the Guildhall in person, you can access this material from home on the internet. The complete indexes can be searched by surname at a cost of £10.00 per family name. You can also purchase the indexes on microfiche and CD. This is certainly a good idea bearing in mind that misspellings often occurred and names change over time.

A good example of this can again be found in my own ancestry. The first waterman in my family was recorded as John Gleghorne. This then became Leghorne, followed Leghon before finally ending up as Legon.

From the perspective of the family historian, the key thing is that if your ancestor worked on the river, (in the area under the jurisdiction of the Company), he will be in the Bindings Indexes. To work on the river, you had to be a member of the Company of Watermen & Lightermen, and indeed to display your badge with your licence number.

The other key piece of information is the location. This is the vital clue to enable further research. A location of, for example, Wapping, suggests that the vital records of the whole family, possibly for generations, are to be found within that geographic area. It is not unusual to find that the same family lived in the same few streets for centuries. Most watermen and lightermen lived close to the Thames.

From 1759 onwards the Apprenticeship Bindings Indexes are supplemented by Apprenticeship Affidavits, (MS6291). This was the attestation that the apprentice was of at least 14 years of age. The Affidavit recorded the apprentice's date of birth, date of baptism and parish of baptism. This is a further vital clue as to which parish registers to search, (parish registers being the prime source of information before Civil Registration started in 1837).

From 1865 onwards a system was introduced for the licensing of over-age 'boys'. Watermen & lightermen that were too old to serve a full apprenticeship were able to obtain a licence by being articled for a period of two years, (MS19548A). This usually meant over the age of 21.

The Company also recorded many other items. The Quarterage records (MS6401), for example, are particularly of use to the family historian. These recorded, for each quarter of the year, payments to the Company for membership, addresses or moorings, and dates of death.

Other records include:

- Records of ferry services, which recorded the names and charges of ferrymen

- Registers of lighters, passenger boats and barges, with names of owners and their plying place or mooring.

- Records of the regulation and disciplinary proceedings of the Company, including the Court of Complaint, (MS6303). This dealt, for example, with the numerous complaints of the watermen's use of foul language.

- Records of pensions paid were also kept and survive. MS6400 yielded that from April 1794 to July 1797, Grace Legon was paid a pension of five shillings and sixpence. It then notes her death.

- Records of watermen in the Navy (MS8911), 'When last heard from by their relatives'.

- List of members killed in the navy (MS6385), early 19th century.

- Book of copies of protections for Company officials, their servants and ferrymen protected from impressment, with ages, physical descriptions and addresses (MS8910).

- Table of rates, prices and fares limited and fixed by the Court of Aldermen. (MS6382). Issued 15th July 1828.

The Corporation of Trinity House also licensed watermen. These were drawn from the ranks of ex-mariners, usually older in age than the normal apprenticeship age. Only one register (MS30335), covering the period 1829-64 survives.

With the information gathered from the Apprenticeship Bindings Indexes, the Affidavits and the other Guildhall sources you can then further your research.

Civil Registration

For dates after Civil Registration started on 1st July 1837, birth, marriage and death certificates can be obtained. These are indexed into quarterly periods for each year, January to March 1850, for example. The indexes can be searched online at such sites as www.findmypast.com.

Using the dates obtained from the archives of the Company of Watermen and Lightermen, you will very quickly be able to locate your ancestors in the indexes. Make note of the reference number shown. You will then be able to apply for the relevant certificates.

The information shown on the various certificates is as follows.

Birth certificates
- child's forenames
- gender
- date of birth
- place of birth
- mother's full name and maiden name
- father's full name and occupation (if married to the mother)
- name, address and relationship to the child of the person who registered the birth.

Marriage certificates
- date of marriage
- place of marriage
- whether by banns, licence or certificate
- name and age of bride and groom
- occupation of bride and groom
- marital status of bride and groom
- current address of bride and groom
- names and occupations of the fathers of the bride and groom
- names of witnesses.

Death certificates
- full name of the deceased
- date of death
- place of death
- given age
- cause of death
- occupation (or name and occupation of husband if the deceased was a married woman)
- name, address and family relationship of the person reporting the death.

Certificates can be ordered in person, by post and online. (see Appendix X for details).

It is a good idea to purchase a binder to store your certificates in and to keep them organised.

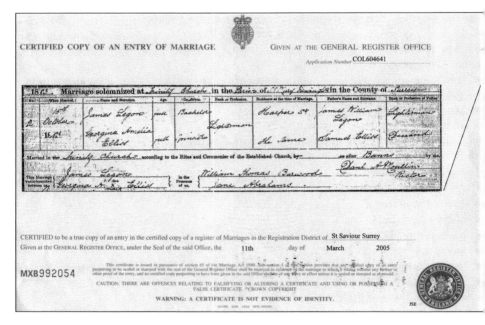

14. Marriage Certificate

Parish Registers

Prior to Civil Registration in 1837 the major source of vital records is likely to be parish registers. These recorded baptisms, marriages and burials.

Your search of the records at the Guildhall will have suggested which parishes your ancestors lived in. The Apprenticeship Affidavit of James Legon, for example, shows that he was baptised on the 15th February 1801 in the parish of St John Wapping.

The London Metropolitan Archives houses Church of England parish registers. (Catholic registers were not deposited and remain in the keeping of the various churches). These are available to search in person on microfilm. In some cases, you can even get to see the original registers.

If you already know the exact date and parish of baptism, it is easy to find the relevant entry. In the printed lists of parishes, organised by Borough, look up the relevant church and note the number of the roll of microfilm.
When you already know the exact date of baptisms, take the microfilm straight to a reader/printer, pay the fee, and obtain a printout.

The information that you can usually expect to find on a parish register varies enormously. Generally speaking, the further back in time you go, less information was recorded. I have frequently been asked in my capacity as a transcriber "why isn't there a date of birth recorded in the entry?". What you have to bear in mind is that it was not the job of the church to record dates of birth. The church was concerned with recording the event of baptism. The fact that so many baptism entries do record a date of birth should be regarded as a bonus.

The information typically found in a 19th century parish register is as follows.

Baptisms
- date of baptism
- date of birth, (sometimes, but not always)
- child's forenames
- names of the father and mother
- surname
- address, (sometimes an exact street address, often just the name of the parish)
- occupation or status of the father
- the name of the parish clerk or curate recording the entry

Marriages
- the year of marriage
- the place of marriage, including the parish and county
- register entry number
- the date of the marriage
- name and surname of groom and bride

- age of groom and bride
- condition (e.g. bachelor, spinster, widow, widower)
- rank or profession (occupation) of both
- residence at the time of marriage (both groom and bride)
- father's name & surname (of both groom and bride)
- rank or profession of father (of both groom and bride)
- whether by banns, or licence
- signatures of the groom and bride (or their marks)
- signatures of two witnesses
- signature of the person performing the ceremony.

Burials
- name of the parish
- name of the county
- year of the death
- name of the deceased
- abode
- date of burial
- age
- signature of the person performing the ceremony.

(Please note: ages given in these records are not always accurate and should always be treated with a pinch of salt!). Sometimes mention might also be made of the cause of death.

Once you have obtained the printouts for the baptisms for which you have an exact date, things get a little trickier. As mentioned previously, the odds are that if there is one ancestor in a parish register, there are likely to be a whole lot more.

At this stage, I would strongly advise taking a step back and reviewing the evidence so far accumulated. From the previous research at the Guildhall, you should now have a list of parishes with which your ancestors are connected. Refer to the parish map in the Readers room and make a note of all the parishes adjacent to the ones you have noted. Also, note when the parish came into existence.

Consider most carefully the recording of what registers you will be searching and note accurately the precise periods searched. This will save much duplication of effort later.

Having got yourself organised, you can begin your search of the registers. Some, but by no means all, have been indexed and this certainly saves time. The downside though is that you are relying on the accuracy of the transcription. There is no guarantee that the original entry will appear in the index. For this reason, I personally prefer to ignore indexes and instead concentrate on searching the original registers.

Searching through the registers is a time consuming process. You can spend an entire day looking at one roll of microfilm and not reach the end. Much depends on the condition of the original written register at the time of microfilming. Much also depends on the legibility of the writer. And just as you get to understand a particular writer's style of handwriting, the writer changes!

Some of these films go back for hundreds of years. My search of St Paul Shadwell for example, covered the years 1670 to 1904. Whilst in the later years entries were recorded in pre-printed forms, the earlier years consisted of closely written lines on foolscap paper. A good quality magnifying glass often comes in handy.

So, in addition to the details already gleaned from the Watermen archives, you should now be able to find the waterman's brothers and sisters, parents, ancestors and descendants.

By this stage you will no doubt have constructed a family tree.

The International Genealogical Index (IGI), can be of much use for those searching online. This was a project initiated by the Church of Jesus Christ of the Latter Day Saints and it recorded many parishes. Unfortunately, not all! Also, not all of the entry was recorded; the occupation and address for example were not included.

It was due to these omissions, both in parishes and in detail, that I myself became involved in the transcription of parish registers. A growing number of these east end of London parish registers can be found on my website at www.parishregister.com

Other transcribers, most notably Robert Cottrell, have also transcribed many of the Thames parishes where Watermen and Lightermen resided. Many family history societies have also published their own transcriptions.

The McLaughlin guide 'Parish Registers' covers this topic in depth.

Census

The information obtained so far can be further supplemented by the various census records. A census has been carried out every 10 years and the details made public after 100 years. The most useful ones for the family historian begin in 1841 and culminate with the 1901 census. The ones between 1801 and 1831 are of little use, recording merely head counts of each household.

The census records, once found at the Family Records Centre on microfilm and microfiche, can now be found at The National Archives (TNA). Searching for these can be a time-consuming process, as much depends on whether you know which street you are looking for and which registration district it is in. At this point, I would refer you to the detailed advice given by TNA, both at Kew and online.

The 1881 census can be searched very easily online, free of charge. The 1901 census is also online, and parts too of the 1861 census. You do have to pay modest charges to use this facility.

The 1841, 1851, 1861, 1871 and 1891 censuses are also now widely available commercially. Companies such as Archive CD Books and Stepping Stones have scanned the original images onto CDs and you can obtain these from my website too.

A typical census return records the following information for each address:

- registration district
- registration sub-district
- address
- names of the occupants
- relationship to the head of the household, e.g. son, servant, lodger
- age
- gender
- marital status
- birthplace
- if disabled, the nature of the disability.

Sometimes you might not find what you are expecting to find. What has to be borne in mind is that the census recorded the actual location on the day of the census, not the occupants of a house. Thus, if great grandmother Mabel is not listed, she might perhaps have been visiting a relative or in a hospital or it might be a clue that she had already passed away.

Also, the census registration district does not necessarily always correspond with county boundaries.

For a greater understanding on this subject I found the book 'Making Use of the Census' by Susan Lumas of much use.

Having now searched the major sources of the occupation records, civil registration records, parish registers and the censuses you should have a pretty extensive amount of information. The bones of your family tree should now be in place.

Wills-After 1858

Wills proved from 12th January 1858 to the present day are kept by the Court of Probate. These can be accessed and purchased from the Court in person (see address in Appendix V).There is also an index to wills, called the National Probate Calendar, on microfiche and microfilm. This can be accessed at the National Archives, the Guildhall Library and at the Society of Genealogists.

If you know the exact date of death, you can buy copies of wills by post.

Many Wills for the County of Middlesex can be accessed online using the LMA's website. These cover the period 1608-1810, (with some gaps).

The information that can be found is as follows:

- name
- parish
- occupation
- description of bequests
- names of executors
- date of the will
- signatures of witnesses

Wills-Before 1858

The National Archives holds records of the Prerogative Court of Canterbury (PCC). You can view these in person and online. The PCC dealt mainly with the wills of the very wealthy. You are more likely to find details of your ancestors in one of the minor probate courts. These records are held in your local county record office.

For an in depth look at this subject I would recommend the excellent guides *Wills and other Probate Records* by Karen Grannum and Nigel Tayler (TNA 2004) or *Probate Jurisdictions* by Jeremy Gibson and Else Churchill (FFHS 2002).

Family History Societies (FHS)

These are another invaluable source of information. Once you have identified the geographic area(s) that your ancestors lived in, it is well worth considering joining the FHS that covers that area. As most watermen and lightermen lived close by the Thames I have listed below some of the Societies that cover the Thames area. Addresses and contact details can also be found at the end in Appendix V.

- East of London FHS (EoLFHS)
- North West Kent FHS
- Essex Society for Family History
- Woolwich FHS
- East Surrey FHS
- London Westminster and Middlesex FHS
- West Middlesex FHS.

Family History Societies undertake many transcriptions not found elsewhere. The EoLFHS, for example, has the St George in the East Land Tax Assessment and this microfiche yielded that a James Legon resided in Churches Gardens in 1801. MS 6341 at the Guildhall recorded that he lived at number 2 Churches Gardens in 1803.

National Archives (N.A.)

As mentioned in the first chapter, there exists at the N.A. a 1628(9) Admiralty Muster of watermen. (SP 16/135,[4]). It was compiled as part of a national register for naval impressment. This lists the names of about 2,400 men, together with their age in 1628(9) and their location. It also lists the number of voyages they had been on and noted any special skills they had, (Quarter Gunner, for example).

This Muster is particularly important to the family historian as it pre-dates the Fire of London and the beginning of the records of the Company of Watermen and Lightermen. The oldest person in it, William Board of Kingston, is listed as being 98 years old, giving a date of birth in 1531.

It seems likely that it lists all of the waterman of that time, including the rulers, masters and apprentices.

The N.A. holds many other useful sources pertaining to watermen and Lightermen.

Houses of Parliament

The Company of Watermen and Lightermen was set up and governed by Act of Parliament. It is not surprising therefore that many records which make reference to watermen survive.

Throughout their long history, the Company were also frequently petitioning Parliament. The subjects of impressment and bridge building in particular incurred their wrath.

Of particular use to the family historian is a petition of 1648 (HL/PO/JO/10/2/11). This lists the names of nearly 2,500 watermen, again, including the rulers, masters and apprentices. It too appears to be a complete listing of all the watermen, the numbers tallying with the earlier Admiralty Muster of 1628(9).

It's significance is that it provides a vital link between the earlier Muster and the later beginnings of the Apprenticeship Bindings in 1692. Thus, some lucky people are going to be able to trace ancestors from the 20th century back as far as the 16th century.

Case Study: Legon Watermen and Lightermen

The starting point of this case study will be familiar to many family historians. My aunt, Mrs Patricia Shaw, mentioned that her father 'did something on the river'. Being young at the time, I was not that interested. Towards the end of her life, she gave me a family tree that a relative had given her. Now this did arouse my curiosity, as I had grown up being told that my brothers and I were the last people to bear the name Legon.

An afternoon at my local library looking in telephone directories quickly put paid to that notion. There were dozens of entries, all over the country.

The family tree that my aunt gave me only had a dozen or so names on it, but it did go back several generations. I had now reached that point familiar to many of you reading this: A burning desire to know who my ancestors were and to find out how far back in time it would be possible to go.

Unfortunately, my father was completely in the dark concerning our ancestry but he too said that his father had worked on the Thames. He also said that the family had come from the east end of London.

Several years previously, my aunt had also given me my grandfather's watch and his wallet. I had put these away and forgotten all about them. On opening the wallet, I found a vital piece of evidence: A Waterman's Licence, dated 1943. Here was proof positive that my grandfather had indeed worked on the river Thames. Magically, my sister-in-law also gave me his Apprenticeship Binding which had been hanging on her wall for years.

I had recently acquired my first computer, together with internet access. I typed the words 'Thames waterman' into a search engine and was surprised by the great amount of material displayed. Right away, I saw that the Guildhall Library had records of the Company of Watermen and Lightermen, going back centuries.

I was soon on my way to the Guildhall, by now thoroughly excited. On arrival I spoke to the helpful staff and was given a set of microfiche containing images of the transcribed Apprenticeship Bindings to look at. I started with the newest one first and lo and behold, there was my grandfather! Apprenticed 9th March 1911, to another James Legon, in a place called St George in the East, Stepney. Not only that, there were another three Legon entries; the same names that were on the family tree.

A short while later, I had searched through all the bindings indexes on microfiche. What I found astounded me. There were thirty eight entries in total, the first dated 1717. I then found the entries on the rolls of microfilm and printed out copies.

After subsequently searching the Apprenticeship Affidavits not only did I have records of the working lives of all these people, I also had their dates of baptism and most of their dates of birth. Crucially, the research made it clear that they all came from the Shadwell/Wapping/Stepney and Bermondsey/Rotherhithe areas.

It quickly became obvious that the trade had been passed down from father to sons, all the time living in the same few streets. I was now able to expand on the tree that my aunt had given me. Having started my search knowing just about my father and grandfather, I now had a tree that went back nine generations.

I also found that the name had changed over the years. Much to my amazement, back in 1701 it was spelt Gleghorne, then Leghorne before finally ending up as Legon. This put paid to another family myth.

Having identified the parishes mentioned, in the Bindings Indexes, I set out for the London Metropolitan Archives (LMA) to search the relevant parish registers. I started out by searching, from beginning to end, each of the parishes mentioned in the Guildhall records. Firstly the baptism registers, then the marriage and burial registers.

As a self employed gardener and it being winter, I was fortunate to have some time on my hands. Just as well, because searching all those registers was an almost daily task for a period of about three months.

From the microfilm and in some cases the original registers, I now had the details of about six hundred people. The tree now had long ago left the realms of a single piece of paper and I was seriously considering the merits of a family tree as wallpaper!

I then moved on to searching the census records and purchased the 1881 census. This added detail, such as addresses and picked up other ancestors whom I had not found in the parish registers. I did the same with the London 1891 census. This took a lot longer as it is not as user friendly as the 1881.When the 1901 census finally came online I was able to extend my knowledge further into the 20th century.

For records from 1837 onwards, (the beginning of civil registration), I was able to obtain birth, marriage and death certificates. I used the website www.findmypast.com to obtain the appropriate reference numbers and applied to the Family Records Centre for the certificates. I only applied for the certificates of my direct ancestors and for those whom I knew existed from the censuses but could not find in the parish registers.

I did use the International Genealogical Index but only as a finding aid. It was useful to identify which parishes to search. This was because the IGI makes no mention of addresses or occupations.

It is not the purpose of this guide to be the complete Legon family history, nor to detail each and every record. I have included below however some of the highlights in order to show what it is possible to find out.

An abbreviated family tree is shown in Appendix IV

Although the formal period of Apprenticeship was seven (later five) years, it is not uncommon to find much longer periods recorded. This could be for many reasons. One amongst these was when the hapless apprentice was impressed into the Navy. This was a practice that had flourished since the 14th century. It was usually the apprentices who were impressed and not the masters, as they were younger and stronger.

Port of London Authority.

No. 37155

WATERMAN'S LICENCE to 31st December, 1943

This is to Certify that the Port of London Authority hereby Re-License

James William Legon

354 Mortlake Road Kynd Essex from the date hereof until the 31st December, 1943, to work as a Waterman in the navigation of Row Boats, Sailing Boats, Steam Boats, and Vessels on all parts of the River Thames, between the landward limit of the Port of London and Lower Hope Point, near Gravesend, in the County of Kent, and in or on all Docks, Canals, Creeks, and Harbours of, or out of, the said River, so far as the tide flows therein, and have granted him a Number for this Licence, which Licence and Number have been duly registered as required by Law. This Licence is liable to be revoked, suspended, or cancelled at any time, by the Port of London Authority, for misconduct or incompetency.

Dated this *Seventh* day of *January* 1942

A. C. Higgins Secretary.

This Licence must be returned to the Registration of Craft and Licensing Office of the Port Authority, Trinity Square, E.C.3, on or before the 31st December, 1943. Any person acting as a Waterman without a Licence, or after the Licence has expired, or refusing to produce the same to any Officer of the Port Authority, or other Waterman producing a Licence, or using this Licence other than the person to whom it is granted, is liable to a penalty of £5.

15. Waterman's Licence

---

his Indenture Witnesseth, That *James William Legon* Son of *James Legon*

of the Parish of *Bow*

in the *County of Middlesex*

doth put himself

Apprentice to *James Legon*

of the Parish of *aforesaid*

in the County *aforesaid*

a Freeman

of the Company of Watermen and Lightermen of the River Thames.

1514—1859.

to learn his Art, and with him (after the manner of an Apprentice) to dwell and serve upon the River of Thames from the Day of the Date hereof until the full End and Term of ___ years from thence next following, to be fully complete and ended; during which Term the said Apprentice his said Master faithfully shall serve as aforesaid, his Secrets keep, his lawful Commandments every where gladly do; He shall do no damage to his said Master nor see it to be done by others, but that he to his Power, shall let or forthwith give Warning to his said Master of the same; He shall not waste the Goods of his said Master, nor lend them unlawfully to any; He shall not commit Fornication nor contract Matrimony within the said Term; He shall not play at Cards, Dice, Tables, nor any other unlawful games whereby his said Master may have any Loss. With his own Goods, or others, during the said Term, without Licence to his said Master he shall not buy nor sell; He shall not haunt Taverns nor Play-Houses, nor absent himself from his Master's Service Day nor Night, unlawfully, but in all things as a faithful Apprentice he shall behave himself towards his said Master, and all his during the said Term. And the said Master in consideration of the ___

his said Apprentice in the same Art which he useth by the best means that he can, shall teach and instruct, or cause to be taught and instructed, finding unto the said Apprentice Meat, Drink, Apparel, Lodging, and all other Necessaries according to the Custom of the City of London. And for the true Performance of all and every the said Covenants and Agreements, each of the said Parties bind themselves unto the other by these Presents. IN WITNESS whereof the Parties above named in these Indentures interchangeably have put their Hands and Seals.

Dated ___ Day of ___

Signed and Delivered, at Watermen's Hall, London, in the Presence of

Members of the Court.

James William Legon

Clerk.

N.B.—The Indentures must bear date the day they are executed; and if any Money is given or contracted for with the Master and Apprentice, the same must be inserted in Words at full length in the body of the Indentures, and the Duty thereon paid by the Master to the Stamp Office, in London, within One Month after the execution thereof, under a Penalty of Fifty Pounds, and double the amount of the Premium given and the Indentures become void.

16. Apprenticeship Binding of John Leghorne 1717, MS6289 Guildhall Library

The following is an extract from my grandfather's binding, dated 9th March 1911:

" This Indenture witnesseth that James William Legon son of James Legon of the Parish of Bow, in the County of Middlesex doth put himself Apprentice to James Legon of the Parish of Aforesaid in the County of Aforesaid a Freeman of the Company of Watermen and Lightermen of the River Thames .To learn his Art, and with him (after the manner of an Apprentice) to dwell and serve upon the River of Thames from the Day of the Date hereof until the full End and Term of Seven years from thence next following, to be fully complete and ended; during which Term the said Apprentice his said Master faithfully shall serve as aforesaid, his Secrets keep, his lawful Commandments every where gladly do; He shall do no damage to his said Master nor see it to be done by others, but that he to his Power, shall let or forthwith give Warning to his said Master of the same; He shall not waste the Goods of his said Master, nor lend them unlawfully to any; He shall not commit Fornication nor contract Matrimony within the said Term; He shall not play at Cards, Dice, Tables, nor any other unlawful games whereby his said Master may have any Loss. With his own Goods, or others, during the said Term, without License or his said Master he shall not buy nor sell; He shall not haunt Taverns nor Play-Houses, nor absent himself from his Master's Service Day nor Night, unlawfully, but in all things as a faithful Apprentice he shall behave himself towards his said Master, and all his, during the said Term. And the said Master in consideration of the Services of his said Apprentice in the same Art which he useth by the best means that he can, shall teach and instruct, or cause to be taught and instructed, finding unto the said Apprentice Meat, Drink, Apparel, Lodging, and all other Necessaries according to the Custom of the City of London. And for the true Performance of all and every the said Covenants and Agreements, each of the said Parties bind themselves unto the other by these Presents. IN WITNESS whereof the Parties above named in these Indentures interchangeably have put their Hands and Seals."

The document is then signed by two of the Members of the Court and by the Apprentice and Master. Wax seals were then applied, and a fee of two shillings and sixpence paid.

17. Freedom from impressment pass

Amongst the treasures unearthed in the search for my watermen ancestors was this entry from a register (MS8911) recording those watermen granted freedom from impressment passes. I love the part which states that he 'wears his own hair'!

18. Parish register marriage entry

This is the record of my great great great great grandfather's marriage to Susannah Butler on Christmas day 1799. He was the first Legon to bear the name James. This was found in the marriage registers of St John Wapping (Ref x089/160).

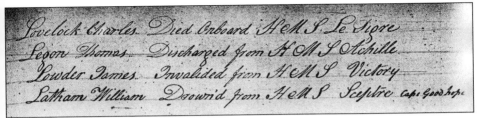

19. Register of watermen in the Navy

Taken from a register of watermen in the Navy, (MS 6386), Thomas Legon was discharged from HMS Achille in 1800.

20. Quarterage records

The above records are taken from the Quarterage records, (MS6401). It shows the payment records of twelve Legon watermen in the early to mid 19th century. It lists their location, numbers, names and the quarter of the year.

Another interesting discovery was found in MS6400. This recorded pensioners of the Company. My great, great grandfather, James William Legon, was paid a pension of 10s 9d between August 1896 and November 1910.Presumably he was paid it till he died, in 1917 at the grand old age of 87.

BIBLIOGRAPHY AND FURTHER READING

History of the Origin & Progress of the Company of Watermen & Lightermen of the River Thames, by Henry Humpherus, published by EP Microform,1981, ISBN 0715853503, hardback, 508 pages. If your interest is the Watermen's Company, this is the definitive book on the subject. Humpherus was a clerk to the Company and this book was originally published between 1874 and 1886. This was a three volume version, covering the years 1515-1859, some 1340 pages in all. Both the three volume work and the 1981 edition are available from Waterman's Hall. The 1981 edition contains a new introduction by the 1978 Master of the Company, John Constant. This can also be read at the Guildhall Library.

Thames Watermen in the Century of Revolution by Christopher O'Riordan, 1992. http://www.geocities.com/thameswatermen/contents.htm Whilst Humpherus remains the first port of call for anyone with a serious interest in the Company of Watermen & Lightermen, this book adds flesh to the somewhat dry bones of Humpherus' work.

All the Works of John Taylor the Water Poet by John Taylor, published by Scolar P, 1973, ISBN 0854179976, hardcover 632 pages. John Taylor was a member of the ruling elite of the Company and Clerk to the Company in 1642. His works have contributed much to our knowledge of the life of Watermen in the 17th century.

Voices from the Waterways by Jean Stone, published by Sutton Publishing Ltd., 2000. ISBN 0750923857. Paperback. Chapter 7 features Robert Crouch, Bargemaster to HM the Queen until 1997, a 3rd generation Watermen and winner of Doggett's Coat & Badge in 1958. Wonderful recollections of a life on the river.

Tales of a Thames Lighterman by Ernest G. Murray, published by Baron Birch for Quotes Ltd.,1992, ISBN 0860235157, hardback,136 pages. Written by a former lighterman, this book tells the story of life on London's river. From his earliest recollections of childhood at the turn of the century to the demise of the docks in the 80's. This is the definitive book on what it took to pass your Apprenticeship and gain the Freedom of the Company of Watermen. Unfortunately no longer in print, but sometimes available 2nd hand. Expect to pay over £30 for the hardback edition. Well worth trying your local library.

London River-The Thames Story by Gavin Weightman, published by Collins & Brown Ltd, 1990 ISBN 1855850753, hardcover 160 pages. This is the story of London's great waterway, based on sources ranging from the latest evidence unearthed by archaeologists, to the first-hand memories of the people whose lives were on the river. Lavishly illustrated.

Men of the Tideway by Dick Fagan and Eric Burgess, published by Robert Hale, 1966. ISBN B0000CMZDB hardback 186 pages. Dick Fagan, a Freeman for over 40 years, shares his memories of a life working afloat. The photographs vividly illustrate both the times and the work on London's river.

From Sussex Yeoman to Greenwich Waterman by A.W.Gearing, published by Country Books, 2001, ISBN: 1898941556, paperback ,176 pages.

Under Oars: Reminiscences of a Thames Lighterman, 1894-1909 by Harry Harris, published by Centerprise Trust, 1978, ISBN: 090373835X, paperback, 42 pages.

Working Lives Volume 1 1905-1945: A People's Autobiography of Hackney published by Hackney WEA with Centerprise Publishing Project, undated, ISBN: 090373821X, card covers 127 pages. Includes the contribution from a lighterman, Alfred Dedman.

Dockland Life: A Pictorial History of London's Docks 1860-2000 by Chris Ellmers and Alex Werner, published by Mainstream Publishing Company (Edinburgh) Ltd, 1991, ISBN 1840183187, hardback, 221 pages. This is the main book for a photographic recollection of London's Docks.

Dockland: Illustrated Historical Survey of Life and Work in East London, R J M Carr (Editor). Paperback 304 pages (March 1986). Publisher: GLC. ISBN : 0716816113. Features an interview by Chris Ellmers with a Lighterman, John Jupp.

On the River: Memories of a Working River Edited by Pam Schweitzer and Charles Wegner, published by Age Exchange Theatre Trust, 1989, ISBN 0947860096, paperback, 184 pages.

The Coat: The Origin and Times of Doggett's Famous Wager, by Bob Crouch, published by Trafford Publishing, Canada (6 Sep 2005), ISBN 1412055288, paperback, 266 pages.

Enter the Press-Gang: Naval Impressment in Eighteenth-Century British Literature, by Daniel James Ellis, published by University of Delaware Press, 2002, ISBN 0874137551, hardback, 219 pages.

Travel in England in the Seventeenth Century, by Joan Parkes, published by Greenwood Press; New edition (Oct 1970), ISBN 083714308X, hardback, 354 pages. (Chapter 4, section 'River Travel', pp.96-110, in particular provides a good background to the working life and conditions of the watermen).

Ancestral Trails by Mark D Herber published by Sutton Publishing, 2004, ISBN: 0-7509-4198-7, 840 pages.

Wills and Other Probate Records by Karen Grannum and Nigel Taylor published y The National Archives, 2004, ISBN: 9781903365496, 220 pages.

Making Use of the Census by Susan Lumas, published by The National Archives, 2002, ISBN 9781903365359, paperback, 128 pages.

GLOSSARY

Affidavit:	Attestation by an apprentice of his date of birth.
Beadle:	Officer of the Company who challenged watermen for their licence to enforce the rule that only licensed watermen worked on the river. Also checked a master's credentials at the binding ceremony.
Binding Date:	Date of commencement of an Apprenticeship
Bumboat:	The 'floating Tesco' of the Thames; small boats that sold everything including vegetables, rope, sail cloth, beer and pitch.
By:	A buoy.
Call-on:	The system of selection of men for casual work.
Cargo:	The goods carried in a ship.
Chalkies:	Nickname for lightermen from the Gravesend, Northfleet and Dartford areas.
Company:	The Company of Watermen and Lightermen of the River Thames.
Dock:	A man made structure enclosing water where ships are loaded, unloaded or repaired.
Dock company:	A company that runs or owns a dock or several docks.
Docker:	Person who loads/unloads ships from the shore.
Docker's case hook:	An S shaped metal hook with a wooden handle.
Drop down:	Row down river.
Dry dock:	Structure to hold a ship out of water for repairs.
Export dock:	A dock where the goods are loaded onto ships for shipping abroad.
Freedom:	Term used when an Apprentice had completed his Apprenticeship, becoming a Freeman of the Company.
Freeman:	A member of the Company, admitted after serving his Apprenticeship and passing his examination.
Free water clause:	The exemption from charges for a lighter entering a dock to load/unload a ship.
Great frost:	A freeze-up of the river.
Humping:	Stowing a barge by carrying sacks on the back.
Import dock:	A dock where the ships unload goods from abroad.
Labour master:	Employed by the lighterage company to allocate work to the lightermen.
Lighter:	Type of barge used by a Lightermen
Lighterman:	Involved in 'lightening' a ship of its cargo, either for unloading ashore, or transferring to another ship

Long ferry:	Type of barge used for transporting a lot of passengers.
Master/Mistress:	The person formally responsible for the Apprentice
On the stones:	Unemployed.
Paddles:	Oars used on a punt. Twenty five feet long.
Plying place:	Place on the river bank where watermen waited for passengers.
Poker:	Lightermen confined to work inside the docks.
Pound:	Stretch of water between two locks on a canal.
Port of London Authority: (PLA)	The organisation since 1909 that is responsible for the Port, the running of the docks and of the Thames tidal waterway.
Punt:	Lighterman's barge, carrying up to fifty tons of cargo.
Quarterage:	Payment of "dues" by a Freeman of the Company, on a quarterly basis.
Quay:	Landing place where ships are unloaded or loaded. Usually made of stone or metal.
Roads:	Cluster of barges moored between two buoys.
Royal Waterman:	Waterman in the service of the monarchy.
Rulers:	Elected officials of the Company
Sailor-man:	Thames sailing barge.
Sculler:	A waterman using one oar in a wherry.
Shallop:	Thames rowing boat manned by 6 or 8 liveried oarsmen.
Shooting off:	Casting off from a tug while being towed.
Shooting the bridge:	The act of navigating the turbulent water under a bridge, whilst avoiding collision with the bridge abutments.
Skiff:	A later development of the wherry. It was a smaller craft with a transom or flat stern.
Slacker:	Winding handle on a lock sluice.
Slang:	A watch chain.
Stairs:	Places where Watermen plied for trade.
Stevedore:	Somebody who works aboard a ship loading and unloading cargo.
Tallying:	Process of counting the cargo loaded into a lighter.
The Bridge:	London Bridge
Tickling:	Lightening of a boat by sanding down the planks
Tijin:	A night's work. Also known as a dark-un.
Tilt-boats:	Boats having a 'tilt' or awning.
Transit shed:	Used for short periods to store goods before they are loaded or after they have been unloaded.
Upstream docks:	Those lying eastwards of Tower bridge.

Up through:	Taking a barge under oars up river through the bridges.
Warehouse:	A building used for the storage of goods.
Waterman Hoy!:	Greeting used by Watermen on the River
Waterman:	Rowed passengers, typically in a wherry.
Wet dock:	Dock containing water, as opposed to a dry dock.
Wharf:	A platform built on the shore or out into the water used for loading/unloading ships.
Wharfinger:	The owner of a wharf.
Wherry:	Type of boat used by a Waterman. 22.5 feet average, seating up to five people.
Whig:	In the late 17th century the term Whig was used to describe those opposed to the religious policies of Charles II.

APPENDICES

Appendix I Masters of the Company

1827 Francis Theodore Hay (1st Master)
1828 John Drinkald
1829 Anthony Lyon
1830 Robert Thomson
1831 Joseph Turnley
1832 Thomas East
1833 Robert Banyon
1834 William Easton
1835 William Randall
1836 Charles Hay
1837 Charles J. White
1838 John Drew
1839 James J. Thompson
1840 John Raymond
1841 Thomas Young
1842 Henry Hobbs
1843 Francis Flower
1844 John Addis
1845 John Dudin Brown
1846 Thomas Groves
1847 Richard Robbins
1848 W. W. Landell
1849 Samuel Pocock
1850 Webster Flockton
1851 John Newell
1852 Clement Peache
1853 George Cooper
1854 Charles Lucey
1855 Henry Grey
1856 Joseph Turnley
1857 William A. Joyce
1858 Charles H. Thompson
1859 William C. Raymond
1860 William Downing
1861 Thomas White
1862 Thomas Pillow
1863 Francis Sales

1864 John Downey
1865 William Tomlin
1866 Thomas Pillow
1867 John R. Berry
1868 William Bromley
1869 William Winn
1870 William Winn
1871 William S. Page
1872 Joseph Lucey
1873 William T. Bond
1874 Samuel Williams
1875 John D. Lee
1876 Richard Cory
1877 John Gaywood
1878 Thomas W. Elliott
1879 George Ward
1880 Richard Phillipps
1881 William S. Hinton
1882 Joseph J. Smith
1899 Sales, Arthur
1900 Sales, Arthur
1901 Sales, Arthur
1902 Keep, Harry
1903 Keep, Harry
1904 Deering, Richard
1905 Williams, W. Varco
1906 Williams, W. Varco
1907 Murray, Sidney G.
1908 East, Richard W.
1909 Philip, Frederick
1910 Philip, Frederick
1911 Alder, Gilbert
1912 Jacobs, Thomas W.
1913 Clements, James
1914 Spicer, Edward A.
1915 Alder, George
1916 Taylor, Edwin W.

1917 Clements, James
1918 Spicer, Edward A.
1919 Stratford, John T.
1920 Goldsmith, Edward J.
1921 Brown, Leonard J.P.
1922 Jacob, Reginald
1923 Scoulding, John T.
1924 Pearce, William
1925 Clayton, Forrester
1926 Higgs, Harry B.
1927 Catt, Harry Jacob
1928 Bailey, William P.
1929 Bryan, Robert M.
1930 Williams, F.Ainslie
1931 Gradner, Frank
1932 Wrightson, William L.
1933 Perfect, Charles T.
1934 Coulton, William
1935 Scanlan, William C.
1936 Philip, Reginald E.
1937 Francis, Reginald R.
1938 Francis, Reginald R.
1939 Brown, Leonard J.P
1940 Rogers, Harry
1941 Etheredge, Charles D
1942 Etheredge, Charles D
1943 Braithwaite, Charles T.
1944 Braithwaite, Charles T.
1945 Collard, Henry L.
1946 Collard, Henry L.
1947 Goldsmith, Edward J.K.
1948 Wright, Robert G.
1949 Lines, Walter J.B.
1950 Whitehair, Sydney G.
1951 Odell, Richard G.
1952 Hardee, Harry D.
1953 Taylor, John B.
1954 Brown, Geoffrey A.
1955 Locket, Frank B.
1956 Williams, A.Lawrence
1957 Philip, Ian E.

1958 Stratford, Jack
1959 Metcalfe, Sir Ralph
1960 Sudbury, Frederick A.
1961 Sudbury, Frederick A.
1962 Locket, Frank B.
1963 Robottom, H. Percival
1964 Burnett, Sir David H. Bt
1965 Marriott, William H.
1966 Page, John A.
1967 Denny, Alderman Sir Lionel
1968 Shelbourne, C.P.
1969 Gasell, Auriol S.
1970 Gilman, H.J.
1971 Sargent, Robert M.
1972 Clarabut, David S.
1973 Woodward-Fisher, K.N.
1974 Collard, Geoffrey L.
1975 Garrett, Geoffrey E.
1976 Francis, Malcolm R.
1977 Cunis, Ryan A.
1978 Constant, John
1979 Metcalf, T.J. Tertius
1980 Spong,S .E. Alan
1981 Braithwaite, C.P.
1982 Rawson, Alderman Christopher
1983 Rawson, Alderman Christopher
1984 Clark-Kennedy, Alec C.
1985 Piper, D.J.(Peter)
1986 Peacock, Sir Geoffrey
1987 Crouch, Robert G.
1988 Turk, Michael J.
1989 Adams, John G.
1990 Mack, H. Graham
1991 Crowden, James G.P.
1992 Woods, Alan T.
1993 Roberts, Peter D.T.
1994 Badcock, Julian K.
1995 Allen, David
1996 Edge, Captain Sir Malcolm
1997 Jenkinson, Jeffrey. MVO
1998 Livett, Christopher J.

1999 Johnson, James G.
2000 Barrow, Lionel G.
2001 Newens, Charles G.
2002 Allan, John S.
2003 Lupton, Robert E.
2004 Benson, Sir Christopher

2005 Benson, Sir Christopher
2006 Howard, Andrew
2007 Wheeler, Brian
2008 Dwan, Kenneth

Source: Company of Watermen and Lightermen

Appendix II Winners of Doggett's Coat & Badge Race

(year won, name, district)

1716 Bishop, E, or Guildford E.
1717 Not known
1718 Not known
1719 Dolby, J. Rotherhithe
1720 Not known
1721 Gurney, C. Foxhall
1722 Morris, W. Rotherhithe
1723 Howard, E. Capers or Cupids Bridge
1724 Not known
1725 Not known
1726 Barrow, T. Sunbury
1727 Not known
1728 Gibbs, J. St Mary Overy
1729 Bean, J. Steel Yard
1730 Broughton, J. Hungerford
1731 Aliss, J. Battersea
1732 Adams, R. Masons
1733 Swabey, W. Whitehall
1734 Bellows, J. Black Lion
1735 Watford, H. Temple
1736 Hilliard, W. Westminster
1737 Heaver, J. Battersea
1738 Oakes, J. King's Arms
1739 Harrington, G. St Saviours
1740 Winch, J. Whitefriars
1741 Roberts, D. St Mary Overy
1742 Not known
1743 Wood, A.

1744 Polton, J. Marigold
1745 Blazdell, J.
1746 White, J.
1747 Joyner, J. Beer Quay
1748 Wagdon, T. Whitefriars
1749 Hilden, H. Mills Stairs
1750 Duncombe, J. Blackfriars
1751 Earle, J. Irongate
1752 Hogden, J
1753 Sandiford, N. Masons Stair
1754 Marshall, A. St Saviours
1755 Gill, C. Old Swan
1756 Not known
1757 White, J. Purley
1758 Danby, J. Christ Church
1759 Clarke, J. Blackfriars
1760 Wood, E.
1761 Penner, W.
1762 Wood, W.
1763 Egglestone, S. Pauls
1764 Morris, J. Horseferry
1765 Egglestone, R. St Catherines
1766 Not known
1767 Not known
1768 Watson, W. Westminster
1769 Not known
1770 Goddard, T. Greenwich
1771 Badman, A. Queenhithe
1772 Briggs, H. Somerset

1773 Frogley, J. Marigold
1774 Not known
1775 Not known
1776 Price, W. Mills
1777 Pickering, J. Greenhithe
1778 Pearson, H.J.B. Lambeth
1779 Boadington, W. Brickwell Point
1780 Bradshaw, John J. Pickle Herring
1781 Reeves, W. Not known
1782 Trucke. Tower
1783 Bowler, James. Not Known
1784 Davis, John. Queenhithe
1785 Not Known Not Known
1786 Nash, James. King Stairs, Horsleydown
1787 Rawlinson, B. Bankside
1788 Radbourne, Thomas. Wandsworth
1789 Curtis, J. Not Known
1790 Byers. Not Known
1791 Easton, Thomas. Old Swan
1792 Kettleby, James. Westminster
1793 Haley, Abraham. Horseleydown
1794 Franklin, James. Putney
1795 Parry, William. Hungerford
1796 Thompson, James. Wapping, Old Stairs
1797 Hill, James. Bankside
1798 Williams, Thomas. Ratcliffe Cross
1799 Dixon, John. Paddington
1800 Burgoyne, John. Blackfriars
1801 Curtis, John Robert. Queenhithe
1802 Burns, William. Limehouse
1803 Flower, John. Hungerford
1804 Gingle, Charles. Temple
1805 Johnson, Thomas. Vauxhall
1806 Goodwin, John. Ratcliffe Cross
1807 Evans, John A. Mill Stairs
1808 Newell, George. Battle Bridge
1809 Jury, Francis. Hermitage
1810 Smart, James. Strand

1811 Thorton, William. Hungerford
1812 May, Richard. Westminster
1813 Farson, Richard. Bankside
1814 Harris, Richard. Bankside
1815 Scott, John. Bankside
1816 Tenham, Thomas. Blackfriars
1817 Robson, James. Wapping Stairs
1818 Nicholls, William. Greenwich
1819 Emery, William. Hungerford
1820 Hartley, Joseph. Strand
1821 Cole Senr., Thomas. Chelsea
1822 Noulton, William. Lambeth
1823 Butcher, George. Hungerford
1824 Fogo, George. Battle-Bridge
1825 Staples, George. Battle-Bridge
1826 Poett, John. Bankside
1827 Voss, James. Fountain Stairs
1828 Mallett, R. Lambeth
1829 Stubbs, S. Old Barge House
1830 Butler, William. Vauxhall
1831 Oliver, R. Deptford
1832 Waight, Robert. Bankside
1833 Maynard, George. Lambeth
1834 Tomlinson, William. Whitehall
1835 Dryson, William. Kidney Stairs
1836 Morris, James. Horselydown
1837 Harrison, Thomas. Bankside
1838 Bridge, Samuel W. Kidney Stairs
1839 Goodrum, Thomas. Vauxhall Stairs
1840 Hawkins, William. Kidney Stairs
1841 Moore, Richard. Surrey Canal
1842 Liddey, James. Wandsworth
1843 Fry, James. Kidney Stairs
1844 Lett, Frederick. Lambeth
1845 Cobb, F. Greenwich
1846 Wing, John F. Pimlico
1847 Ellis, William H. Westminster
1848 Ash, John. Rotherhithe
1849 Cole, Thomas. Chelsea
1850 Campbell, William. Westminster

1851 Wigget, George D. Somers Quay
1852 Constable, Charles. Lambeth
1853 Finnis, James R. Tower
1854 Hemmings, David J. Bankside
1855 White, Henry J. Mill Stairs
1856 Everson, George W. Greenwich
1857 White, Thomas C. Mill Stairs
1858 Turner, Charles J. Rotherhithe
1859 Farrow, Charles S. Mill Stairs
1860 Phelps, Henry J.M. Fulham
1861 Short, Samuel. Bermondsey
1862 Messenger, John Cherry Garden
  Stairs
1863 Young, Thomas. Rotherhithe
1864 Coombes, David. Horseleydown
1865 Wood, John W. Mill Stairs
1866 Iles, Arthur. Kew
1867 Maxwell, Henry M. Custom House
1868 Egalton, Alfred. Blackwall
1869 Wright, George. Bermondsey
1870 Harding, Richard. Blackwall
1871 MacKinney, Thomas J. Richmond
1872 Green, Thomas G. Hammersmith
1873 Messum, Henry. Richmond
1874 Burwood, Robert W. Wapping
1875 Phelps, William. Putney
1876 Bulman, Charles T. Shadwell
1877 Tarryer, John. Rotherhithe
1878 Taylor, Thos. E. Hermitage Stairs
1879 Cordery, Henry. Putney
1880 Cobb, William J. Putney
1881 Claridge, G. Richmond
1882 Audsley, H.A. Lambeth
1883 Lloyd, J. Wandsworth
1884 Phelps, C. Putney
1885 Mackinney, J. Twickenham
1886 Cole, H. Deptford
1887 East, W.G. Richmond
1888 Harding, C.R. Chelsea
1889 Green, G.M. Lambeth
1890 Sanson, J.T.G. Chiswick

1891 Barry, W.A. Victoria Docks
1892 Webb, G. Gravesend
1893 Harding, J.Jnr. Chelsea
1894 Pearce, F. Hammersmith
1895 Gibson, J.H. Putney
1896 Carter, R.J. Greenwich
1897 Bullman, T. Wapping
1898 Carter, A.J. Greenwich
1899 See, J. Fulham
1900 Turffrey, J.J. Bankside
1901 Brewer, A.H. Putney
1902 Odell, R.G .Lambeth
1903 Barry, E. Wandsworth
1904 Pizzey, W.A. Lambeth
1905 Silvester, H Hammersmith
1906 Brewer, E.L Putney
1907 Cook, A.T. Hammersmith
1908 Graham, J. Erith
1909 Luck, G.R. Erith
1910 Pocock, R.J. Elton
1911 Woodward Fisher, W.J. Millwall
1912 Francis, L.E. Kingston
1913 Gobbett, G.H.J. Greenwich
1914 Mason, S.G. Charlton
1915 West, L.P.J. Wapping
1916 Pearce, F.W. Hammersmith
1917 Blackman, J.H. Gravesend
1918 Gibbs, A. Richmond
1919 Phelps, H.T. Putney
1920 Hayes, H. Deptford
1921 Briggs, A.E. Ratcliff Cross
1922 Phelps, T.J. Putney
1923 Phelps R.W. Putney
1924 Green, H.C. Poplar
1925 Barry, H.A. Barnes Bridge
1926 Green, T.G.M. Mortlake
1927 Barry, L.B. Herne Hill
1928 Phelps, J.L. Henley
1929 Taylor, C.F. Blackwall
1930 Phelps, E.L. Henley
1931 Harding, T.J. Putney

1932 Silvester, H.T. Hammersmith
1933 Phelps, E.L. Putney
1934 Smith, H.J. Gravesend
1935 Gobbett, A.E. Blackwall
1936 Taylor, J.A. Gravesend
1937 Silvester, W.F. Hammersmith
1938 Phelps, E.H. Putney
1939 Thomas, D.E. Dagenham
1940 Lupton, E.G. Northfleet
1941 Bowles, G.D. Isleworth
1942 Dott, F. Erith
1943 McGuiness, E.F. Greenwich
1944 Ambler, F. E., Twickenham
1945 Thomas, S., Dagenham
1946 Amson, J. D., Northfleet
1947 Palmer, J. V., Gravesend
1948 Clark, H. F., Ilford
1949 Dymott, A. H., Gravesend
1950 Palmer, G. J., Gravesend
1951 Martin, M. J. A., Upminster
1952 Green, G. E., Putney
1953 Bowles, R. E., Brentford
1954 Everest, K. C., Hornchurch
1955 Goulding, J. T., New Cross
1956 Williams, C.. Deptford
1957 Collins, K. C., Downham
1958 Crouch, R. G., East Greenwich
1959 Saunders, G. L., Erith
1960 Easterling, R. W., Lee
1961 Usher, K. R., Limehouse
1962 Dearsley, C. A., North Woolwich
1963 Alien, D., Erith
1964 Walker, F. F., Eltham
1965 Collins, A. G., Bromley
1966 Stent, D., Eltham
1967 Briggs, C. M., East Ham
1968 Lupton, J. E., Gravesend
1969 Grieves, L. E., Mile End
1970 Spencer, M. S., Greenwich
1971 Dwan, K. V., Gravesend

1972 Wilson, P., Catford
1973 Prentice, R. A., Wapping
1974 Lupton, R. E., Gravesend
1975 Drury, C. M., Battersea
1976 Prentice, P., Wapping
1977 Dwan, J., Dartford
1978 Macpherson, A. L., Poplar
1979 Burwood, F. J., Plaistow
1980 Woodward-Fisher, W.R. Battersea
1981 Hickman, W. D, Greenwich
1982 Anness, G. B., West Ham
1983 Hickman, P. J., Charlton
1984 McCarthy, S. J., Blackheath
1985 Spencer, R. B., Rainham
1986 Woodward-Fisher, C.J.,
   Westminster
1987 Spencer, C., Dagenham
1988 Hayes, G. A., Mottingham
1989 Humphrey, R.A., Blackheath
1990 Collins, S. C., Rotherhithe
1991 Neicho, L. C., Sevenoaks
1992 McCarthy, J. J., Blackheath
1993 Clifford, J. D., Gravesend
1994 Bullas, C., Higham
1995 Neicho, S., Isle of Dogs
1996 Coleman, R. G., Ladywell
1997 Russell, M. J., Gravesend
1998 Bushnell, D. J., Wargrave
1999 Woods, T.W., Wapping
2000 Rickner , B., Greenwich
2001 Beasley, N., Barking
2002 Dwan, N. R., Swanley
2003 Cairns, M.G, Greenwich
2004 Dwan, R.E, Swanley
2005 Dean, Jack, Medway
2006 Hunter, Ross
2007 McGrane, Jude

Source: Company of Watermen and Lightermen

Appendix III Plying places and wharves on the Thames

North Shore

Twickenham (Wharf Lane)
Twickenham (Water Lane)
Twickenham (Queen's Head)
St Margaret's Ferry
Church Ferry Stairs
Chiswick Ferry
Bishops Park Upper Stairs
Cricketers Stairs (Chelsea)
Adelphi (Fox-under-the-Hill) Stairs
Temple Stairs
Custom House (Lower) Stairs
Tower Stairs
Irongate Stairs

New Crane Stairs
Pelican Stairs
Shadwell Dock Stairs
Stone Stairs
Ratcliffe Cross Stairs
Limehouse Hole Stairs
Torrington Arms New Stairs
Blackwall Stairs
North Woolwich Stairs
Purfleet Causeway
Union Stairs
Wapping Old Stairs

South Shore

Lambeth Stairs
Upper (St Thomas) Stairs
Morgan Lane Stairs
Horselydown New Stairs
Fountain Stairs
Cherry Garden Stairs
Rotherhithe (Platform) Stairs
Princess Stairs
Elephant Stairs
Church Stairs
Hanover Stairs

Globe Stairs
Cuckolds (Horn Stairs)
St George's Stairs
Upper Watergate Deptford Stairs
Garden Stairs
East Greenwich (Bugsby's Hole) Stairs
Erith Stairs and Causeway
Greenhithe (Conservancy) Causeway
Gravesend Town quay
Gravesend New Bridge Causeway

Source: Company of Watermen and Lightermen.

Wharves of the river Thames

Fresh Wharf*
London Bridge Wharf
Nicholson's Wharf
Custom House Quay
Irongate Wharf
Carron and Continental Wharves
Downe's Wharf**
Black Lions Wharf**
Black Eagle Wharf
Hermitage Wharf
Morocco and Eagle Wharf
Free Trade Wharf
Dundee Wharf
Fenning's Wharf***
Sun Wharf***
Topping' Wharf***
Cotton's Wharf
Chamberlain's Wharf
Hay's Wharf

Stanton's Wharf
Symon's Wharf
Gun & Shot Wharf
Mark Brown's Wharf***
Butler's Wharf
Platform Wharf
Platform Sufferance Wharf
National Wharf
Corbett's Wharf
Trinity Buoy Wharf
Cyde Wharf
Tate's Wharf
Plaistow Wharf
Anchor & Hope Wharf
Lett's Wharf
Phoenix wharf

Source: www.portcities.org.uk

  *   Later New Fresh Wharf
 **   Later London and Continental Wharf
***   All later part of Hay's Wharf

Appendix IV Abbreviated Family Tree of the descendents of John Gleghorne Watermen & Lightermen* of the River Thames

John Gleghorne = 1701 Hannah Didcot
c1680-1730
St Paul, Shadwell
|
Thomas Leghorne = 1725 Grace Tailor
1703-1747
St Paul, Shadwell
|
Charles Legon = 1757 Isabella Bubb
1729-
St Paul, Shadwell
|
James Legon = 1799 Susannah Butler
1772 –1825
St Paul, Shadwell
|
James William Legon = Sarah
1801-1857
St John, Wapping
|
James William Legon = 1850 Mary Ann Hilliard
1830-1917
St George in the East
|
James William Legon = 1883 Georgina Amelia Ellis
1865-1930   1864-1919
St George in the East
|
James William Legon = 1922 Alice Amelia Kelly
1895-1969   1902-1982
St Peter, London Docks
|
James Legon = 1960 Shirley Kay Wright
1934-   1935-
Dagenham
|
James William Legon = 1992 Isabelle Logerot
1961-   1963-
West Ham   = 2004 Yvonne Lee
                             1957-

James Kwok-Hai Lee- Legon	Talisa Eva Legon
1988	1992
Harlow	Walthamstow

* Watermen &
Lightermen in bold.

55

Appendix V Useful Addresses & Websites

Waterman's Hall
16 St Mary-at-Hill
London EC3R
Tel: 020 7283 2373
Website:www.watermenshall.org
Email: clerk@watermenshall.org

Guildhall Library
Manuscripts Section
Aldermanbury
London EC2P 2EJ
Tel: 020 7332 1863
Website: www.history.ac.uk/gh/ghaccess.htm
Email: manuscripts.guildhall@corpoflondon.gov.uk

London Metropolitan Archives
40 Northampton Road
London EC1R 0HB
Tel: 020 7332 3820
Website:www.cityoflondon.gov.uk/Corporation/leisure_heritage/libraries_archives_
museums_galleries/lma/lma.htm
Email: ask.lma@ms.corpoflondon.gov.uk

Society of Genealogists
14 Charterhouse Buildings
Goswell Road
London EC1M 7BA
Tel: 020 7251 8799
Website: www.sog.org.uk
Email: genealogy@sog.org.uk

Docklands Ancestors Ltd.
15 Honeycroft
Loughton
Essex IG10 3PR
Website: www.ParishRegister.com
Email: docklandsancestors@parishregister.com
The author's website, featuring Watermen & Lightermen, a Picture Gallery, Parish
Register Transcriptions, Message Forum, Research Services and Online Shop.

Robert J. Cottrell
Trueflare Ltd
Sudbury
New Barn Road
New Barn
Longfield
Kent DA3 7JE

Website :http://hometown.aol.com/rjcindex/trueflare.html
Email : rjcindex@aol.com

East of London Family History Society
New Memberships Secretary
37 Medora Road
Romford RM7 7EP
Website : www.eolfhs.org.uk
Email : See website

Museum in Docklands
No 1 Warehouse
West India Quay
Hertsmere Road
London E14 4AL
Website : www.museumindocklands.org.uk
Email : info@museumindocklands.org.uk

www.portoflondon.co.uk
Website of the Port of London Authority. Interesting section on the history of the port
of London, Thames Bridges, Rowing on the Thames and Doggett's Coat and Badge
Race.

www.shipbrook.com/jeff/boatfare.html
Jeff Lee's webpage showing fare rates c1555 and landing places.

www.findmypast.com
Civil Registration birth, marriage and death entries online.

www.geocities.com/thameswatermen/index.htm
Christopher O'Riordan's excellent and authoritative history of the Watermen's
Company. Essential reading!

http://collage.cityoflondon.gov.uk/
Corporation of London's image gallery.

www.britishpathe.com/index.html
Website of British Pathe News.

www.portcities.org.uk/london/server/show/nav.001002001
Portcities contains much detail on docklands, the Thames and maritime history. Also, a photograph of twenty Doggett's Coat and Badge winners.

Appendix VI Timeline of the River Thames

1st century AD	-	Romans arrive in London. First bridge built.
2nd century AD	-	Londinium well established as a port. Birth of the lighterage industry.
c900	-	Ethelredshithe quay founded
1078	-	Work starts on the Tower of London
1176	-	Work began on the first stone London Bridge
1193	-	Corporation of London appointed Conservator of the Thames
1206	-	First stone London Bridge completed
1370	-	First regulations governing watermen passed
1513	-	Henry VIII established Royal Dockyards at Woolwich and Deptford and founded Trinity House to oversee pilotage and collect dues on the Thames
1514	-	Further regulation of watermen's charges
1551	-	Opening of the first Legal quays
1555	-	Further regulation of watermen
1566	-	Company of Watermen formed by Act of Parliament
1585	-	Company granted arms by Elizabeth I
1614	-	East India Company founded a wet dock at Blackwall
1651	-	Hay's Wharf founded
1665	-	Great Plague
1666	-	Fire of London; Waterman's Hall destroyed
1670	-	Waterman's Hall rebuilt on same site
1696	-	First dock built. Howlands Wet Dock, later known as Greenland Dock, then as part of the Surrey Commercial group.
1700	-	Lightermen join the Company of Watermen
1715	-	First Doggett's Coat and Badge Race
1721	-	Third Waterman's Hall erected on site of second
1750	-	Westminster Bridge opened
1751	-	Shipping canal-the Limehouse Cut opened
1759	-	First Kew Bridge opened
1760	-	Carron Ironworks opens in Wapping
1769	-	Blackfriars Bridge opened
1780	-	Company of Watermen move to present day Hall
1789	-	Second Kew Bridge opened
1790	-	Brunswick Dock opened
1798	-	Thames Police established
1801	-	Grand Surrey Canal begun
1802	-	West India Dock opened

1805	-	London Dock opened
1806	-	East India Docks opened, formerly known as Perry's Dock
1807	-	Commercial Dock Company buys Greenland Dock (formerly the Great Howland)
1809	-	Baltic Dock opened; first of the new Surrey docks
1811	-	East Country Dock opened
1817	-	Waterloo Bridge opened, (formerly Stand Bridge)
1820	-	Regent's Canal completed
1825	-	New London Bridge started
1827	-	Company of Watermen & Lightermen Incorporated by Act of Parliament
1828	-	St Katharine's Dock opened
1831	-	London Bridge replaced (this is the bridge sent to Arizona in the 1960s)
1842	-	Thames Tunnel opened
1846	-	Irongate wharf destroyed by fire
1846	-	Thames Ironworks opened
1849	-	Barnes Bridge opened
1855	-	Royal Victoria Dock opened
1858	-	Great Eastern built at Millwall
1860	-	HMS Warrior built at Blackwall
1860	-	Westminster Bridge opened
1860	-	Grosvenor (Victoria) Bridge opened
1864	-	Blackfriars Railway Bridge opened
1868	-	Millwall Docks opened
1869	-	Woolwich and Deptford Dockyards closed, the Royal Navy having built larger yards elsewhere.
1873	-	Albert Bridge opened
1880	-	Royal Albert Dock opened
1886	-	Tilbury Docks opened
1889	-	The Great dock strike
1894	-	Richmond Lock footbridges opened
1894	-	Tower Bridge opened
1895	-	Thames Ironworks Football Club formed-later West Ham FC
1897	-	Blackwall Tunnel opened
1903	-	Third Kew Bridge opened
1906	-	Vauxhall Bridge opened
1909	-	Port of London Authority established
1911/12	-	Further dock strikes
1912	-	Thames Ironworks & Shipbuilding Company closes
1917	-	The Silvertown explosion

1917	-	Tilbury Docks extended
1921	-	King George V dock opened
1933	-	Chiswick Bridge opened
1940-41	-	The Blitz brings severe damage to the docks
1945	-	New Waterloo Bridge opened
1947	-	National Dock Labour Board introduced
1960s	-	Major expansion at Tilbury Docks
1967	-	End of casual work
1970s	-	Further expansion of Tilbury ; Northfleet Hope Container Terminal opened
1973	-	New London Bridge opened
1968-71	-	St Katharine's, London and Surrey Commercial Docks close
1967-71	-	Hay's and all the other major wharves close
1976-81	-	West India, Royal Docks and Millwall Docks close
1981	-	London Docklands Development Corporation founded to redevelop the derelict dockland areas
1984	-	Thames Barrier opened to prevent flooding
1987	-	Docklands Light Railway opened
1991	-	Queen Elizabeth II Bridge opened at Dartford
2000	-	Millennium Bridge opened and immediately closed for repairs!
2002	-	Millennium Bridge reopens

Appendix VII Lighterage Companies

Company	*Location/Note*
Aldridge Thomas & Sons	Galley Quay, Lower Thames Street; Trinity Chambers, Water Lane, Tower Street, and 311 Wapping High street
Allen Bros. and Transit Company Ltd	62 Bridge Street, Greenwich
Anderson & Dean Ltd.	
Badcock's	
Beaumont, W.J., Lighterage Ltd	
Beckett Bros, 83 Lower Thames Street, EC	
Bells and Taylor	Fresh Wharf, 2 Lower Thames Street
Berry & Edwards	Curtis & Harvey's Wharf, Church Street, Isleworth
Betts J. & B	5 Cross Lane, St Mary-at-Hill, and Botolph Wharf
Blackfriars Lighterage and Cartage Co Ltd	Cousin Lane, Upper Thames Street EC
Blackston Jos. & Son	Shad Thames
Blewett Benjamin Granger & Co	Cox's Quay, Lower Thames Street; Jerusalem Coffee House, Cowper's Court, Cornhill; Coldharbour, Blackwall
Bradley, Edward	Bridge Wharf, Church Street, Isleworth
Braithwaite & Dean Ltd.	
Bridge, William & Sons	Pier Wharf, 122 Church Road, Battersea
Brown & Young	19 Thomas Street, Horselydown & 82 Bermondsey Wall
Buck & Son Ltd	172 High Street, Brentford
Buck, Alf & Son	172 High Street, Brentford
Burgess J & W	29 Horselydown Lane
City of London Lighterage Company, Ltd.	
Clark & Sons	6 Tower Dock
Clements Knowling & Co Ltd	Brentford

Clements, Jas. & Co	63 High Street, Brentford
Collier, Geo. Hy. Ltd	94 High Street, Brentford
Commercial Lighterage Co	Free Trade Wharf, Ratcliff
Cooks, J.W. & Co. Ltd.	Tilbury Docks
Coombe & Marsh	53 Great Tower Street
Cory Lighterage	Coal & rough goods
Cory Tank Lighterage Co.	Division of Cory Lighterage
Cory, Wm. and Son Ltd	52 Mark Lane, EC
Covington & Co	26 Nicholas Lane, 1 Warkworth Terrace, Commercial Road East & 27 Wharf Road, City Road
Covington, Henry	Railway Wharf, Victoria Road, Battersea
Dagenham Lighterage Company	Dagenham Docks
Darling Brothers	
Downs (Edwin), Kennedy & Co	St Helena Wharf, Waterside, Richmond
Downs Edwin & Co	St Helena Wharf, Waterside, Richmond; & at 70 New Corn Exchange, Mark Lane, London
Drinkald John & Sons	19 Beer Lane
Dudin, Hen & Sons	East Lane, Bermondsey Wall; Springall's Wharf, Bermondsey Wall; Jerusalem Wharf, Shad Thames & Commercial Sale Rooms, Mincing Lane
Dunkin C & Lee	Horselydown
Dunkin Hen. & John	Davis's Lower Wharf, Potter's Fields, Horselydown & 5 Old Corn Exchange
Erith & Dartford Lighterage Co	High Street, Erith
Everitt & Cookes	53 Lower Thames Street
Everitt, Wild & Co	Lower Thames Street
Ferndale Lighterage	
Fielder, Hickman & Co	4 Catherine Court, Seething Lane and 88 Narrow Street, Limehouse
Fisher, Bill	Limehouse
Fosse & Williams	Ord Street, Poplar

Fossett & Sons	52 Lower Thames Street
General Lighterage Co	
Goulding, R & Sons	Potter's Fields
Griffith & Co	5 Maze Hl., Greenwich
Groves, Thos & Sons	Mill Street, Dockhead; Platform Wharf, Rotherhithe Street, a& East Lane
Gunner, John & Son	Tower Wharf, Tower Hill
Hammerton Bros.	6 George Street, Richmond
Harrisons	Coal
Hasler, Robert & Son	5 Old Fish Street
Hawkins, John Messrs.	Lower Road, Rotherhithe
Hay, Charles & Son	57 Rotherhithe Street
Hay, J F & Son	14 Princes Street, Rotherhithe
Hays & Wheeler	20 Mill Street, Dockhead
Henderson & Sons	5 St George's Terrace, Knights Road, Victoria Docks
Higgs	
Hope Lighterage Co Ltd	Goat Wharf, High Street, Brentford
Humphery, Arthur Jun.	Royal Albert Docks
Humphrey & Grey (Lighterage) Ltd	Tilbury Docks
Irongate Lighterage Ltd	
Jones, William & George	Davis's Lower Wharf, Horselydown
Keen & Blake	Northumberland Wharf, New Brentford
Keen & Blake	New Corn Exchange, Mark Lane
Keighley, Fisenden & Co	2 York Terrace, Wharf Road, Kings Cross & 1 Bath Place, William Street, Caledonian Road
Lake, Campbell & Allen	45 Gainsford Street, Horsleydown
Landell & Son	41 Thomas Street, Horselydown
London & Tilbury Lighterage Co	
London and General Steam Tug Lighterage	
London Barge Building and Lighterage Company Ltd.	
Lucas & Company	Lower Thames Street
Lucas Mathias, Prime & John (and agents)	17 Harp Lane, Tower Street
Lucey C & Sons	Cox's Quay, Lower Thames Street

Lucey Widow & Sons	Cox's Quay, Lower Thames Street
Lyon, Jas & Son	Lyon's Wharf, Upper Thames Street
Mackenzie & Grey	20 Colchester Street
Maidlow, Wm & Son	196 Upper Thames Street
Mardlow & Son	196 Upper Thames Street
Marriot Lighterage	
Marsh Jas & Co	53 Great Tower Street
Mercantile Lighterage Co Ltd	Tilbury Docks. Division of Cory Lighterage
Mercantile Lighterage Co Ltd	281 Rotherhithe Street SE
Middlemist & Hammond	82 Lower Thames Street
Moakes, C & Co	Church Street, Battersea
Morpeth Lighterage and Carrying Company Ltd.	
Newell, J & Son	4 Horselydown Lane, & Newell's Wharf, Shad Thames
Page, Samuel & Son	341 Wapping High street
Pells, W. & Son	
Perkins & Broughton	Beaufort Wharf, Beaufort Buildings, Strand
Perkins & Homer	
Phillipps & Grave	Royal Albert Docks
Phillips & Davidson	3 Little Tower Street
Phillips and Groves Lighterage Contractors	23-25 St Dunstans Hill, EC
Phillips Tug and Lighterage Co	
Phillips, Graves & Phillips	11 Rood Lane
Pillow, Thomas & Son	21 Cottage Row & Fountain Stairs, Bermondsey Wall, & 2 Wellington Chambers, London Bridge
Pipers	
Pocock's	
Pomroy & Brandon	George's Stairs, Horsleydown
Pope, William, & Co Ltd	Royal Albert Docks
Pope, Wm & Co	18 Harp Lane, Great Tower Street
Premier Lighterage Towage & Salvage Co Ltd	
Raymond, J & Son	Horseshoe Wharf, Clink Street
Redman & Noehmer	Mill Street, Dockhead
River Lighterage	Coal

Robbins & Miller	Nine Elms, Vauxhall
Ryland & Knight	Shad Thames
Silvertown Services Ltd	
Smith, Son & Smith	3 Upper Thames Street , 50 Marl Lane & 5&6 New Corn Exchange
Soundy & Son	Wood Wharf, Greenwich
South Met	Coal
Speck & Redman	Mill Street, Dockhead
Start Lighterage Co Ltd	
Stutchbury, Jas & Sons	Galley Quay, Lower Thames Street & 37 Seething lane, Tower Street
Styles, Thomas & Sons	Claremont Wharf, Long Ditton, Kingston
Talbot, Robert & Sons	Surrey Docks, Rotherhithe Street
Taylor, E.W & Co	
Taylor, John & Co	Fresh Wharf, Lower Thames Street
Thames and General (Lighterage) Ltd	
Thames Steam Tug & Lighterage Co Ltd	Tilbury Docks. Known on the river as 'Limited'
Thames Steam Tug and Lighterage Co Ltd	Brentford
Thorrington & Roberts	9 Wharf, City Road, Battle-bridge & Kingsland Road
Tough & Henderson Ltd	
Transport and Lighterage Company Ltd.	
Turnley Bros	22 Savage Grounds, Tower Hill
Union Lighterage Co Ltd	Royal Victoria Docks
Vokins & Co	
Watson & Co	White Hart Yard, Tower
West Thurrock Lighterage Co. Ltd.	
West, Benjamin	152 Annandale Road, Greenwich
Whellock, Arthur & Son	42 Great Tower Street & Galley Quay
Whitehair Lighterage Co.	
Wile's	
Williams & Son	9 St Dunstan's Hill
Williams, S. & Sons Ltd	Dagenham Docks
Wingate, W & Son	1 High Street, Battersea
Woodward-Fisher	

Appendix VIII Clerks of the Company 1656-2007

1656-1685	Thomas Lowe*
1685-1686	Richard Allford
1686-1687	Thomas Babenton
1687-1688	Richard Allford
1688-1692	Matthew Webster
1692-1704	Edward Knight
1704-1707	John Glew
1707-1708	E. Knight
1708-1715	John Shooter
1715-1717	John Glew
1717-1723	P. Palmer
1723-1724	Waple
1724-1759	Church
1759-1781	R. Glendoning
1781-1785	J. Cotton
1785-1793	William Dore
1793-1810	William Crage
1810-1811	Thomas Clark
1811-1829	Thomas Shelton
1829-1849	John Banyon
1849-1882	Henry Humpherus
1882-1914	Aubyn Carrick
1914-1947	Barrett Wilson
1947-1986	Andrew Wells
1986-1991	Peter Cameron
1991-1994	Robert Crouch (Past Master)
1997-	Colin C. Middlemiss

*In office that year, may have been appointed earlier.

Source: Henry Humpherus, History of the Origin and Progress of the Company of Watermen and Lightermen of the River Thames and Colin Middlemiss.

Appendix IX Watermen in the Navy c1809 Killed in Action or Invalided

Aldridge	James	Blackmore	William
Allen	Robert	Blakey	Richard
Allen	Thomas	Blandford	Thomas
Allen	William	Bloomfield	William
Allen	William	Blundell	William
Allen	William	Bodfield	Thomas
Anderson	James	Bond	William
Anthony	James	Booth	George
Armstrong	William	Boucher	Joseph Rapley
Arnold	William	Bowie	Alexander
Astie	Charles	Bowie	Francis
Atkins	Thomas	Bowman	William
Atwood	John	Bradshaw	George
Baker	George	Brail	John
Ballantine	Henry	Brazier	Aaron
Bannister	Edward	Brazier	William
Bannister	William	Brazier	William
Barber	Joseph	Brewster	John
Barnard	Robert	Briscoe	Samuel
Barsdale	Thomas	Brittan	Joseph
Bartlett	Robert	Broad	Thomas
Barton	Richard	Brock	Obadiah
Batt	Joseph	Brock	Thomas
Bauld	William	Brookson	James
Bear	George	Brown	James
Beete	Luke	Brown	John
Belighter	James	Brown	John
Bell	George	Brown	John
Bell	Jacob	Brown	John Jnr
Bell	James	Brown	Joseph
Bell	William	Brown	Joseph
Bennett	Charles	Brown	Thomas
Bennett	Robert	Brown	William
Bentley	Thomas	Budd	William
Berry	William	Burck	John
Bevan	James	Burden	George
Bignall	Thomas	Burnett	Charles
Billinosley	William	Burnett	John
Blackmore	Benjamin	Burton	George

Burton	William	Dalrymple	George
Bye	Charles	Dande	James
Cadwell	Samuel	Dark	Edward
Camden	John	Davis	James
Carpenter	Joseph	Davis	John
Carpenter	Richard	Davis	John
Carter	Joseph	Davis	John
Cartwright	John	Davis	Thomas
Carver	William	Davis	W.R
Case	John	Davis	William
Catherall	William	Day	William
Caulvin	Anthony	Dear	William
Challenger	Richard	Dickenson	John
Chant	Isaac	Dickhoff	John
Chapman	William	Dingley	William
Chapman	William	Dowley	Constantine
Christey	John	Drake	George
Clark	James	Dunn	John
Clark	Samuel	Durham	Thomas
Clarkson	David	Durrant	John
Codey	Peter	Eatenton	William
Codner	James	Eatinton	Charles
Cole	John	Edwards	John
Collier	Jeremiah	Edwards	William
Collins	Thomas	Elliott	Richard
Constable	Stephen	Elmore	Robert
Cookson	Thomas	Emmett	[Illegible]
Cookson	William	English	James
Cooper	William	English	James
Corby	Robert	Evans	George
Corne	Edward	Evans	John
Cossington	John	Evenden	Henry
Cotner	Charles	Evenden	John Lane
Court	Joseph	Evenden	William
Cowen	John	Everest	William
Crage	Thomas Tobias	Ewers	Richard
Croker	Benjamin	Farrier	George
Cullen	Alexander	Fehr	William Henry
Currie	James	Fencock	Charles
Curry	Robert	Fenner	George
Curtis	Thomas	Ferguson	Solomon

Ferrett	Edward	Grimes	John
Field	William	Grimley	Uriah
Finch	Edward	Groves	John
Fisher	William	Groves	John
Fletcher	John	Guthrie	John
Forrest	William	Hagley	James
Forster	George	Haines	Thomas
Forster	Peter	Hall	Edward
Francis	Thomas	Hallett	Thomas
Franklin	Matthew	Hamilton	Robert
Free	James	Hampton	Francis
Free	Thomas	Hanson	John
Fuller	John	Hardwick	Samuel
G[Illegible]	Andrew	Hariman	Isaac
G[Illegible]	Edward	Harison	Thomas
Gadd	John Austin	Harris	Henry
Galloway	George	Harrison	William
Gantlett	Thomas	Hart	James
Gardiner	William	Hart	John
Garwood	John	Harvey	Thomas
Gerrard	Joseph	Hawkins	Benjamin
Giles	Charles	Hemmingway	William
Gill	John	Henderson	Robert
Goldhawke	Charles	Henderson	William
Goldhawke	Thomas	Hennis	William
Goldsmith	James	Herbert	Peter
Goodwin	Samuel	Hescott	Henry
Goulding	Thomas	Hill	Joseph
Grace	John	Hinkley	William
Grace	Samuel Smart	Holland	James
Grafton	Henry	Holland	Thomas
Green	Charles	Holligan	William
Green	William	Holloway	John
Greenaway	Richard	Holmes	Anthony
Greenaway	Thomas	Honey	Thomas
Gregory	James	Hopkins	Edward
Gregory	John	Horrod	Thomas
Grey	Samuel	Horsham	John
Grieve	John Alexander	Howlett	William
Griffiths	John	Hubbard	Jonathan
Grimes	James	Hunt	Henry

Huntingdon	Thomas	Littlepage	John
Hushinton	John	Lockey	Alexander
Isbesler	William	Lodge	James
Isdale	Joseph	Lucas	James
Jackson	Richard	Lucey	John
Jackson	Richard	Lucy	John
Jarman	Robert William	Lukes	Jeffery
Jeffries	William	Luxford	John
Jender	Robert	Marley	Henry
Jennett	Joseph	Marriam	[Blank]
Jermaine	James	Marshall	James
Johnson	Charles	Marston	Thomas
Johnson	John	Marston	William [Jnr?]
Johnson	John	Marston	William [Jnr?]
Johnson	Robert	Martell	John
Johnston	Thomas	Martell	William
Jones	John	Martin	John
Jones	John Hiram	Mascoll	Jeremiah
Jones	Joseph	Masterman	Henry
Kellock	Andrew	Masters	Thomas
Kenney	John	May	Thomas
King	William	McClarens	George
King	William	McNeale	Robert
Kitchener	John	Meaton	William
Knight	William	Metcalf	John
Lane	John	Metcalf	Samuel
Lang	Thomas	Middleton	Cades Harder
Latter	William	Middleton	James
Laughton	Peter	Middleton	Thomas Henry
Leadenhouse	Charles	Miller	Thomas
Lear	Charles	Mills	Edward
Leeson	Edward	Mitchell	Edward James
Leeson	William	Molten	Edward
Lefever	Charles	Molten	William
Legg	Thomas	Monday	Thomas
Leggett	William	Moore	Robert
Lenham	John	Moore	William
Leonard	William	Moore	William
Lewington	George	Moss	Thomas
Liddard	[Illegible]	Murdock	Richard
Lipp	John	Myers	Andrew

Myers	William		Place	Henry
Narley	Jeremiah		Planter	Daniel
Nash	William		Pobgee	William
Nichols	George		Poett	John
Nightingale	Thomas		Pollard	Thomas
Norcott	Charles		Pratt	William
Norris	John James		Prescott	Thomas
Nowell	John		Preston	Thomas
Oakley	James		Pullen	Clifford
Oldfield	James		Purdon	John
Oram	Edward		Quittenburn	Henry
Oram	William		Quittenburn	John
Owen	Joseph		Raine	Joseph
Pallin	William		Ralph	Simon
Palmer	James		Randall	James
Parish	Joseph		Randall	Thomas
Parker	James		Ranson	William
Parker	John		Raymond	William
Parker	William		Reed	Thomas
Parr	Jonas		Reffell	George
Parrott	Thomas		Reynolds	Robert
Parsons	William		Richards	Frederick
Pearce	James		Richards	Richard
Pearce	Samuel		Ridgeway	William
Pearce	Thomas		Robinson	James
Pearce	Timothy		Robinson	John
Pendrill	Charles		Robinson	William
Pennell	Michael		Rose	John
Perkins	George		Round	John
Perkins	William		Rumney	Richard
Perriman	John		Rush	John
Perry	Benjamin		Rush	Samuel
Perry	Charles		Rust	Edward
Perry	John		Sansum	John
Perry	Thomas		Satchfield	Thomas
Perry	William		Scott	William
Phelps	Benjamin		Sculthorp	John
Phelps	Peter		Searles	George
Phillips	Lewes		Shaw	Thomas
Philpot	Charles		Sheen	John
Pilley	John		Sheilds	John

Simmonds	Joseph	Taylor	John
Simmons	William	Taylor	William
Sinclair	George	Teague	Edward
Skinner	Thomas	Teasdale	Joseph
Skinner	William	Terry	Thomas
Slaughter	John	Thomas	James
Smith	Benjamin	Thomas	Matthew
Smith	Edward	Thompson	James
Smith	James	Thompson	John
Smith	James	Thompson	William
Smith	James	Thornley	William
Smith	John	Thurston	John
Smith	John	Thurston	William
Smith	John	Tibble	James
Smith	John	Timms	William
Smith	Thomas	Titchgen	George
Smith	William	Townsend	George
Smith	William	Tucker	Joseph
Smock	John	Turner	Benjamin
Soames	John	Turner	Francis
Somerville	William	Turner	Samuel
Sorrell	John	Turner	William Thomas
Sound	William	Twichell	Thomas
Spearing	James	Tyler	Edward
Speight	Richard	Tyler	Thomas
Spendlove	Charles	Underwood	William
Squires	Benjamin	Ungley	John
Stevenson	John Anthony	Upton	George
Stollett	James	Upton	James
Stow	David	Vincent	Benjamin
Stowers	James	Vinney	Richard
Stowers	John	Voss	Joseph
Stowers	Richard	Waghorn	Thomas
Strange	William	Walker	Henry
Strong	John	Walker	John Ashworth
Stronghill	Thomas	Walker	Thomas
Strutton	Benjamin	Wallis	Samuel
Tanner	James	Walter	James
Tate	Clevering	Ward	Joseph
Taylor	Charles	Ware	Robert
Taylor	John	Waters	Thomas

Watson	Henry	Wild	William
Watts	William	Williams	Hugh
Webb	John	Williams	Thomas
Webber	Thomas	Willmot	Samuel
Wennscott	William	Willson	Francis
West	John	Willson	Thomas
West	Leonard	Winter	Charles
West	Sam	Winter	James
Wheatley	Thomas	Winter	William
Wheeler	George	Wise	William
Whellock	William	Wood	James
White	Edward	Wood	John
White	Francis	Wood	William
White	George	Wood	William
Whitehouse	Richard	Woodyer	John
Whiteman	John	Wright	Bradford
Widmer	Richard	Wright	John
Wiggins	James	Wyles	William

Appendix X Archives of the Company of Watermen and Lightermen of the river Thames held at the Guildhall Library

MS. 6281

Rulers general entry books, containing detailed accounts (audited) of expenditure and receipts from courts of freedom and binding, including places of abode or moorings, masters' names and dates of commencement of apprenticeships. 1715-1816

Vol 1 1715-1758*
Vol 2 1715-1724
Vol 3 1724-1734
Vol 4 1735-1745
Vol 5 1745-1760
Vol 6 1760-1775
Vol 7 1776-1792
Vol 8 1792-1816

* Summary accounts, including ferry accounts

MS. 6282

Rulers' cash books. 1702-1807.

Vol 1. 1702-1704
Vol 2. 1718-1726
Vol 3. 1758-1807

MS. 6283

Book of disbursements on the company's account. 1797-1807.

MS. 6284

Clerks' account books. 1811-1859

Vol 1. 1811-1826
Vol 2. 1828-1836
Vol 3. 1836-1846
Vol 4. 1846-1859

MS. 6285

Company (cash) account books, classified except vol 1. which is general. 1805-1916

1. 1805-39
2. 1840-55
3. 1856-59
4. 1860-67
5. 1868-81
6. 1881-97
7. 1897-1909
8. 1909-16

See also MS. 6286

MS. 6286

General account books containing cash account 1860-1930, clerk's account 1872-7 and 1886-1930, and church* repair fund account 1887-1930.

1. 1860-67
2. 1868-77
3. 1877-87
4. 1887-97
5. 1897-1906
6. 1906-30

*Church at Penge.

MS. 6287

Court minute and order books. 1700- 1887

1. 1700-1716, mostly courts of rulers and complaints after 1701, with rough minutes 1701-1702 and 1705-1707 and notes of fines 1701-1702; signed.
2. 1707-1732, general courts (of rulers, auditors, comptrollers and assistants) with lists of court officials; fair.
3. 1732-1746, general court; fair.
4. 1735-1741, court of rulers; fair.
5. 1741-1744, courts of rulers and complaints; fair.*
6. 1745-1747, courts of rulers and complaints; fair.
7. 1746/7-1754, general court; fair.*

8. 1759-1775, summary of business in all courts, with notes of audits and elections of officials; fair.
9. 1775-1785, ditto, with lists of court officers.
10. Now MS. 6287C
11. 1785-1793, summary of business in all courts, mostly general courts, with notes of audits and elections of officers, and lists of court officials; draft
12. 1793/4-1810, all courts; signed.
13. 1793-1813, general court with lists of court officials; audits signed; ? latter part draft.**
14. 1808-1813, court of rulers; fair.
15. 1813-1827, general court with lists of court officials; fair.
16. 1827-1839, court of master, wardens and assistants; signed.
17. 1840-1851, court of master, wardens and assistants; signed.
18. 1851-1859, ditto.
19. 1860-1869, ditto.
20. 1869-1880, ditto.
21. 1880-1887, ditto.

* vol 5-7 bound in 1.
** Includes list of ferrymen wanting protection, 1823, including ages and numbers of children.

MS. 6287A

Committee minute book. 1808-1814.

MS. 6287B

Clerks' out letter books. 1829-1850, 1873-1891 and 1898-1914.

1. 1829-1850
2. 1873- 1882
3. 1882-1891 (Indexed)
4. 1898-1908
5. 1908-14

MS. 6287C

Minute book of orders, contracts, bills etc. considering the purchase of an estate of St. Mary at Hill, pulling down the old premises and building the Hall. 1776-1784.
Formerly MS. 6287/10.

MS. 6288

Call books (court of complaint, binding, freedom, fines, etc.) 1808-1845 and 1853-1893.

1. 1808-1812
2. 1812-1817
3. 1817-1822
4. 1822-1827
5. 1827-1830
6. 1831-1835
7. 1835-1840
8. 1840-1845
9. 1853-1859
10. 1860-1867
11. 1867-1875
12. 1875-1884
13. 1884-1893

MS. 6288A

Gravesend call book (binding, freedom and contracts). 1862-1888.

MS. 6289

Registers of apprenticeship bindings, recording declarations of freedom. 1688-1908.

Vol. 1-8,14-21 and 23-24 indexed integrally (vol.8 indexed to 1742 only). Vol. 9-13 in vol.22.

1. 1688-93 (A)
2. 1693-7 (B)
3. 1697-1706 (C)
4. 1706-12 (D)
5. 1712-19 (E)
6. 1719-25 (F)
7. 1725-35 (G)
8. 1735-44 (H)*
9. 1745-56 (I)
10. 1756-69 (K)
11. 1769-82 (L)**

* Defective index : see heading above.
** Page missing – use 6281/6 11 August 1769
See also MS. 6402A for index of masters with references to bindings and turnings over in these registers 1797-1852.

MS. 6289A

Registers of apprentices taken on trial. 1828-1923.

1. 1828-45
2. 1846-59
3. 1860-95*
4. 1895-1923

* Page references are to the register of freeman, MS. 6307/2

MS. 6289B

Loose apprenticeship indentures and miscellaneous items removed from the register books of apprentices taken on trial (MS6289A). 1872-1894

MS. 6290

Registers of freedom admissions (stamp duty books), giving dates of binding (1765-88 and 1805-1927), masters' names (1765-85 and 1815-1927) and places of abode (1765-85). 1765-1927. Incomplete. Vol. 7-19 indexed.

1. 1765-70
2. 1770-75
3. 1783-88
4. 1789-99
5. 1800-15
6. 1805-15
7. 1815-24
8. 1824-34
9. 1834-46
10. 1846-58
11. 1859-65
12. 1865-69
13. 1870-75
14. 1875-81
15. 1881-88
16. 1888-96
17. 1896-1904
18. 1904-15
19. 1915-27

Note: references in these vols. are to the registers of apprentice bindings (MS. 6289)

MS. 6290A

Calendar of freedom admissions, arranged chronologically, giving places of abode, dates of expiration of apprenticeship and registration or badge numbers.* 1802-1814.

* As in MS. 6318 to April 1803 (approx.) as in MS. 6317 thereafter.

MS. 6291

Apprentices' affidavit books, recording dates of birth and places of baptism. 1759-1897. Indexed.

1. 1759-79*
2. 1780-93**
3. 1793-1807
4. 1808-35
5. 1836-66
6. 1867-97

*Rough list for 1779. (Blank for some of 1778)
**Indexed to Sept. 1786 only. From Jan. 1790 mostly gives names only of apprentices.

MS. 6292

Sunday ferry weekly account books, listing ferrymen with payments for work and money earned. 1721-1813

1. 1721-1727
2. 1727-1736
3. 1736-1745
4. 1745-1754
5. 1754-1761
6. 1761-1768
7. 1768-1775
8. 1775-1782
9. 1782-1789
10. 1794-1802
11. 1789-90 and 1802-1805*
12. 1805-1813
13. 1813-1820
14. 1820-1827
15. 1827-1831

* See also MS. 6294A for 1793
For accounts 1715-18, see MS. 6292A.

MS. 6292A

Sunday ferry account book, giving account for each ferry, listing ferrymen and inspectors' names, money earned, and payments for work. 1715-1718.
See also MS. 6292 for later accounts.
Formerly MS. 6293/1

MS. 6293

Rulers' entry books of accounts for court of freedom and binding, giving masters names and places of abode for bindings and dates of expiration of apprenticeship and places of abode for freedom admissions signed to 1774. 1735-1793.

Vol 1. [Now MS. 6292A]
Vol 2. 1735-1746*
Vol 3. 1747-1763
Vol 4. 1764-1793

*See also MS. 6294
Notes: the information in these vols. is included, slightly more briefly, in MS. 6281/4-7.

MS. 6294

Rulers' entry book (fair copy) containing accounts of payments on binding apprentice, and giving masters' names and places of abode. 1740-1746.
[Above entry is crossed out]

See also MS. 6293/2. Quarterage payments. By court date when freedom granted and Quarterage due.

MS. 6294A

Sunday ferry rough account book, listing ferrymen with payments for work and money earned. 1793. See also MS. 6292/11

MS. 6295

Register of apprentice licences*, giving names and addresses of masters and dates of licences and renewals. 1859-1878.

For licences after 1878, see MS. 6316

Note: page references refer to masters' entries in register of freemen, MS. 6307/2.
* Nos 30,000 – 36,752. These are given (for masters) in MS. 6401/4

MS. 6296

Register of watermen protected from the impress, arranged under employers etc, giving ages, places of abode and dates of warrants (1761-1812)
1761-1824. Comp. late 18th century.

MS. 6297

Court books, giving amounts paid for freedom admissions, apprentice bindings and contracts; including dates of completion of apprenticeship and places of abode for freedom admissions; and masters' names and places of abode for apprentice bindings 1796-1922. Also from April 1910, applications for apprentice licenses, and from 1913 applications for licences under Port of London Authority bye laws.

1. 1796-1810*
1a. 1811-27*
2. 1802-15
3. 1810-26**
4. 1816-28
5. 1828-36
6. 1836-47
7. 1848-60
8. 1860-70
9. 1871-80
10. 1880-92
11. 1893-1906
12. 1906-15
13. 141915-22

* Vol. 1. and 1A include names of apprentices bound, references to masters' freedom in register of freemen (MS. 6307/1), registration numbers to 1803 (from MS. 6318) and badge numbers 1803-27 (from MS. 6317)
** Rough book of freedom admissions and apprentice bindings, with receivers' initials.

MS. 6298

Receivers' accounts of payments for freedom admissions and apprentice bindings, giving places of abode or moorings (with references to registers of apprentice bindings (MS. 6289), for freedom admissions in vol.6,8,10,13 and 14; and to registers of freemen (MS. 6307) for masters' freedom, for apprentice bindings in vol.10,13 and 14). 1802-1942.

1. 1802-14 (r)
2. 1802-15 (f)
3. 1814-26 (r)
4. 1815-25 (f)
5. 1826-39 (f)
6. 1827-4 (r)

7. 1839-51 (f)
8. 1841-56 (r)
9. 1851-64 (f)
10. 1857-74 (r)
11. 1865-75 (f)
12. 1875-90 (f)
13. 1875-93 (r)
14. 1893-1911 (r)
15. 1890-1907 (r)
16. 1907-18 (f)
17. 1918-30 (f)
18. 1911-17 (r)
19. 1917-27 (r)
20. 1927-42
Note: r = rough; f = fair.

MS. 6299

"The "Black book", kept for the entry of the names of persons suspected of binding apprentices and not working them. 1814-1881.

MS. 6300

Impress summons books. 1803-1807.

1. 1803
2. 1805-1807
3. 1807

MS. 6301

Complaint books, listing complaints made against watermen for infringing regulations and agreements, using abusive language etc. 1809-1909.

1. 1809-1813
2. 1813-1818
3. 1818-1822
4. 1822-1829
5. 1830-1856
6. 1857-1870
7. 1871-1890
8. 1890-1909

For earlier complaints see MS. 6302 and 6302A.

MS. 6302

Complaint abstract book, called "Finnis book", giving parties, offences and some details of complaints heard. 1802-1806. See also MSS. 6301 and 6302A

MS. 6302A

Complaint abstract book, giving some details of complaints, called "Morton's book". 1803-1807. See also MSS. 6301, 6302

MS. 6303

Court of complaints:- evidence books, stating evidence offered by complainants, defendants and sometimes witnesses. 1811-1909.

1. 1811-1826
2. 1827-1861
3. 1862-1876
4. 1877-1883
5. 1883-1905
6. 1905-1909

MS. 6304

Court of complaints:- account books listing complaints heard at the court and amounts of fines paid. 1st series. 1808-26.

1. 1808-14
2. 1815-1826

MS. 6305

Court of complaints:- account books, listing complaints heard at the court, stating offences, quoting regulations infringed by each offence, and giving amounts of fines. 2nd series. 1856-1902

1. 1856-64
2. 1865-72
3. 1872-1881
4. 1882-1902*

* see MS. 6305A for loose summonses extracted from this volume.

MS. 6305A

Court of complaints: summonses to attend. 1890 and 1899-1909.
Extracted from MS. 6305

MS. 6306

Register of men and apprentices who intend to supply substitutes (by quota) to serve in H.M. Navy, giving ages and physical descriptions, places of abode, and amounts paid. 1812. Indexed

MS. 6307

Register of free watermen. c. 1763-1891.

Vol. 1. Record of watermen who were members of the company between c. 1763 and 1827 (not many from the earliest years), giving dates of freedom, moorings, quarterly references (? To quarterage payments) c. 1800-1828, and note of whether dead (? In 1800); indexed to p.166 (1802) in MS. 6319/2, and arranged after 1800 in chronological order of freedom admissions.

Note: alphabetical arrangement of the same information excluding earliest references and continuing references to 1831 is in MS. 6316A.

Vol. 2. Register of freemen admitted 1827-1891 in chronological order, recording quarterly payments 1828-1891.

Note: references in the following MS are to MS. 6307:- MS. 6289A, 6295, 6297, 6298/10, 13 & 14, 6316, 6401 (alphabetical) – 6403, 6406.

MS. 6308

Registers of lighter numbers, giving names of owners and abodes or moorings and names and types of boats. Mid 18th century to 1867.

Vol. 1.   Mid 18th cent. – 1805 (nos. 1-999)
Vol. 1A Mid 18th cent. – 1805 (nos. 1001-1432)*
Vol. 2   1803-1830 (nos. 1-999)
Vol. 2A. 1803-1830 (nos. 1001-1748)**

Vol. 3.   1827-1863 (nos. 1-999)
Vol. 4.   1827-1863 (nos. 1001-1792)
Vol. 5.   1851-1867 (nos. 1-999)

* Formerly MS. 6314A, includes some occupations and indications of commodity conveyed.
** Formerly MS. 6314/2

Note: references in MS. 6394 refer to Vol. 1 and 14.
For continuation see MS. 6309.

MS. 6309

Registers of barge owners giving names and addresses or moorings of owners and descriptions of barges. 1860-1894. Indexed

Vol. 1.   1860-1890 (A), nos. 1-999
Vol. 2.   1860-1890 (B), nos 1001-1795
Vol. 3.   1884-1893 (A), nos 1-999
Vol. 4.   1884-1894 (B), nos 1001-1886

See MS. 6320 and 6321 for renewal fees MS. 6308.
This entries continues MS. 6308.

MS. 6310

Registers of boats to let out and of bum boats, arranged numerically, giving names and addresses of owners, names and type of boats and dates and   extensions of licences. 1860-1893. Indexed.

Note. The former MS. 6310/1 is now MS. 6310A
See MS. 6313 for earlier licences.

MS. 6310 A

Bum boats book, giving names, ages and addresses of owners and names and types of boats. 1839-1859.
Formerly MS. 6310/1

MS. 6311

Register of licensed passenger boats, arranged numerically, giving name and addresses of watermen or craft owners, types of boats and numbers of passengers permitted, sales of boats, and renewals and cancellations of licences. 1860-1910.
Indexed in MS. 6312

Note: page references refer to register of freemen, MS. 6307/2.
For earlier licences, see MS. 6313.

MS. 6312

Indexes to registers of licensed passenger boats (MS. 6313/1-2 and 6311). 1828-e. 1910.

1. 1828-2. 1848
2. 1860-e. 1910

MS. 6313

Registers of licensed passenger boats arranged numerically, giving types of craft, names and addresses of watermen or craft owners, and numbers of passengers permitted. 1828-1909.
Incomplete.

[1. Now MS. 6313 A]
2. 1828-38*
3. 1838-53*
4. 1853-59
5. 1865-90**
6. 1890/909**

* Indexed to o. 1848 in the MS. 6312/1
** Summary of information in MS. 6311, not giving addresses.
Note: the licence numbers run consecutively in several separate series beginning in 1828, 1834, 1850, 1853, 1866, 1872, 1880 and 1890.
For later licences see MS. 6310 and 6311.

MS. 6313 A

Register of masters' licences, giving names and description of boats, names of owners and physical descriptions of masters 1805-26. 1805-37*.

*Arranged in 2 sectional nos. 1-38, 1805-1826 and 1-38, 1837-1838.
Note. Formerly MS. 6313/1

MS. 6314

Register of watermen, arranged numerically, giving places of abode or moorings. Late 18th century to 1803. Indexed in MS. 6318

See MS. 6315 for later entries.
Note. Former MS. 6314/2 is now MS. 6308/2A

MS. 6315

Register of watermen, arranged numerically by badge numbers, giving addresses 1803-1827.* Indexed in MS. 6317

* The period during which watermen's badges were issued and supposedly worn.
See MS. 6314 for earlier entries.

MS. 6316

Registry of apprentice licences, giving names and addresses of masters and dates of licences and renewals. 1878-1920.

* Renewals to 1915. Formerly MS. 6316.
See MS. 6295 for licences prior to 1878.
Note: page reference in Vol. 1 refer to masters' entries in register of freemen, MS. 6307/2.

MS. 6316 A

Register of free watermen, alphabetically arranged, giving the dates of freedom, moorings and quarterly references (? To quarterage payments). 1776-1831.

Vol. 1. A – L 1776-1829
Vol. 2. N – Z 1776-1829*

* Some references continued to 1831.
Note: a partly chronological arrangement of the same information, including some earlier references, is in MS. 6307/1.

MS. 6317

Register of watermen, arranged alphabetically, giving badge numbers and addresses (this volume contains the same information as MS. 6315, which is arranged numerically). 1803-?1827*.

*The period during which watermen's badges were issued and supposedly worn.
See MS. 6318 for earlier entries.
Note: references in MS. 6290 A, 6297/1 and 1A and 6394 refer to this volume.

MS. 6318

Register of watermen, arranged alphabetically, giving registration numbers and places of abode or moorings (this volume contains the same information as MS. 6314, which is arranged numerically). Late 18th century to 1803.

Note: the registration numbers quoted in MS. 6290 A (calendar of freedom admissions) prior to April 1803 refer to this volume, as do those in MS. 6297/1 and 1A.

See MS. 6317 for later entries.

MS. 6319

Index to register of free watermen (MS. 6307/pp. 1-166), giving places of abode or moorings, c. 1774-1802.
Vol. 1. A-L
Vol. 2. M-Z

MS. 6320

Account books of renewal fees for registered barge owners, arranged chronologically with references to numerical arrangement (MS. 6321). 1861-1909.

Vol. 1. 1861-1874
Vol. 2. 1874-1890
Vol. 3. 1890-1909
Vol. 4. 1909-1910

MS. 6321

Account book of renewal fees for registered barge owners, arranged numerically as in register (MS. 6309) with references to chronological arrangement (MS. 6320). 1861-1889.

Vol. 1. 1861-1874
Vol. 2. 1875-1889.

MS. 6322

Cash books regarding payments for apprentice licences, chronologically arranged, listing apprentices and masters and giving licence numbers. 1863-1900.

Vol. 1. 1863-1873
Vol. 2. 1874-1886
Vol. 3. 1886-1900
Vol. 4. 1900-1915

MS. 6323

Cash book recording payments for licences for boats to be let out and bum boats, chronologically arranged, listing licence holders and giving boat licence numbers and dates of licences. 1863-1909.

MS. 6324

Cash books of barge owners' registration fees, 1863-1910.

Vol. 1. 1863-87
Vol. 2. 1887-1905
Vol. 3. 1905-10

MS. 6325

Petty cash books. 1863-1917.

Vol. 1. 1863-79
Vol. 2. 1879-89
Vol. 3. 1889-1900
Vol. 4. 1900-17

MS. 6326

Sunday ferry quarterly account book, showing total weekly ferry earnings. Audited. 1745-1807.

MS. 6327

Books of plying places between Chelsea and Windsor. 1808-1886.

Vol. 1. 1808-1838
Vol. 2. 1839-1886

MS. 6328

Book of plying places from Greenwich to Yanlet Creek. 1833-1887.

MS. 6328 A

Book of long plying places, Greenwich to Gravesend. 19th Century.

MS. 6328 B

Book of short plying places, London Bridge to Vauxhall, marked to 1813.

MS. 6329

Book of plying places below London Bridge:- south side. 1833-1888/
See also MS. 6412.

MS. 6329 A

Book of short plying places below London Bridge, marked in 1813.

MS. 6375

Book of signed orders, rules and constitutions of the company, made by the court of rulers, auditors and assistants, with orders more particularly for regulating lightermen, approved 27 February 1700/1 by the Court of Aldermen, and 18 March by a chief justice; with amendments relating to an Order in council, 6 September 1704, approved by the Court of Aldermen 19 September and chief justice 10 October.

MS. 6376

Book of signed orders, rules and constitutions of the company, confirmed and signed by a justice of Queen's Bench, 16 April 1708, with table of officers' and watermen's fees, with rules and orders of the court of rulers, auditors and assistants, approved by the Court of Aldermen 28 July 1713 (and signed by a High court judge 28 April 1714), and 1 November 1732.

MS. 6377

Volume containing signed rules and bye-laws for the good government of the Watermen and Lightermen's company of the river Thames, set down by the master, wardens and assistants, 2 April 1828, approved by the court of Mayor and Aldermen, signed by the Town clerk and examined by a High court judge, 10 July 1828. Company's copy of MS. 1357.

MS. 6378

Volume containing signed rules and bye-laws for the government and regulation of the freemen of the Company of Watermen and Lightermen of the river Thames, their widows and apprentices and the boats, vessels and other craft to be rowed or worked by them, set down by court of Major and Aldermen, signed the Town clerk, 15 April 1828, and examined by a High court judge, 10 July 1828. Company's copy of MS. 1356/1.

MS. 6379

Volume containing signed amended rules and bye-laws for the government of the freemen of the Company of watermen and lightermen of the river Thames, their widows and apprentices and the boats, vessels and other craft to be rowed or worked by them, set down by the court of Major and Aldermen, signed by the Town clerk, 29 March 1836, and examined by a High court judge, 5 May 1836. Company's copy of MS. 1356/2.

MS. 6380

Volume containing signed amended rules and bye-laws for the government and regulation of the freemen of the Company of Watermen and Lightermen of the river Thames, their widows and apprentices and the boats, vessels and other craft to be rowed or worked by them, set down by the court of Major and Aldermen, signed by the Town clerk, 29 September 1845, and examined by a High court judge, 22 December 1845. Company's copy of MS. 1356/3.

MS. 6380 A

Draft bye-laws made by the company for the government of watermen, lightermen, barge owners and others... on the river Thames. 1860.

MS.6381

Bye-laws made by the court of the company, 26 June 1860, and approved by the Conservators of the river Thames, 2 July 1860; also supplementary bye-laws, made 27 December 1864 and approved 16 January 1865; and further supplementary bye-laws, made 1 January 1867 and approved 21 January 1867.

MS. 6382

Volume containing general rules and bye-laws made by the court, 27 December 1864, and approved by the Conservators of the river Thames, 16 January 1865.

MS. 6383

List of rulers, auditors, comptrollers, assistants, clerk, beadles, Sunday ferry men and rulers, watermen protected from the impress, arranged under office, and giving ages and some physical descriptions. 1803-1823.

MS. 6384

Alphabetical list of members of the company protected from the impress (including those in MS. 6383), giving descriptions of the employments or appointments which exempted them. Early 19th century.

See also. MS. 6296.

MS. 6385

Alphabetical list of members of the company at sea and supposed to be in the king's service or prisoners in France. Early 19th century.

MS. 6386

Alphabetical list of 105 members of the company killed in action in the Navy, or invalided in that service, naming their ships. Early 19th century.

MS. 6386 A

Book of subscriptions for the purpose of defraying the expenses incurred by the corps of River Fencibles in supplying the men who volunteered to go to Copenhagen with extra clothing and to provide a weekly allowance for such of them as have families, to be paid to their wives every Saturday during the absence of their husbands on that service. 1808.

See also MS. 6434 and MS. 6434A

MS. 6387

Note book of Richard Martin, clerk, concerning courts of apprentice bindings and freedom admissions in the Gravesend district. 1844-1861.

MS. 6388

Beadle's order book, listing persons to be summoned to courts and committees. 1808-1829.

MS. 6389

Sunday ferry annual accounts, listing weekly total receipts and expenses for each ferry, and showing proportions of earnings paid to ferrymen. 1806-1829.

Vol. 1. 1806-1816
Vol. 2. 1817-1829

MS. 6389A

List of ferries, ferrymen, renters and sureties for Sunday working. 1833-1840/

MS. 6389B

Sunday ferry rough account book, listing stations, ferrymen, and receipts. 1784-1786.

See also MS. 6292/9.

MS. 6390

Sunday ferry cash books, listing weekly cash receipts for each ferry and stating who was responsible for the money. 1830-1843.

Vol.1. 1830-1842
Vol.2. 1842-1843*

* Mainly blank.

MS. 6391

List of pensioners admitted, arranged chronologically, giving dates when pensions raised to 1849, 1821-1831.
See also MS. 6392.

MS. 6391A

List of pensioners recommended for relief, giving ages, addresses, and dates of admission. 1810-1900.

MS. 6391B

Miscellaneous blank forms, letters and birth and marriage certificates, formerly loose in MS. 6391A. 19th century.
Paper and parchment, 51 items in folder.
[Duplicates weeded out 14.12.87 now 31 items]

MS. 6392

Alphabetical lists of pensioners admitted. 1794-1837.

Vol.1. rough copy
Vol.2. fair copy, with corrections and showing increases.

See also MS. 6391.

MS. 6393

Calendar of freemen, usually giving dates of birth, lighter numbers (as in MS. 6308) and stating whether dead at time of compilation (c. 1860) 1827-1859.

MS. 6394

Alphabetical list of members of the company, giving places of abode or moorings, lighter* or badge ("woodmongers") numbers**, with a note of watermen serving at sea, giving names of ships (continued to 1808). 1803.

* See MS. 6308/1.
** See MS. 6317.

MS. 6395

Account books of payments to pensioners, alphabetically arranged within localities. 1742-1760.

1. 1742-1747
2. 1748-1755
3. 1756-1760

For later accounts, see MS. 6400.

MS. 6396

Account books relating mainly to the poor of the company:-
Disbursements on poor accounts 1796-1807
Disbursements and receipts on poor accounts 1805-59*, and record of cash received from individuals and ferries 1843-59.
Disbursements and receipts on poor account 1860-75; also record of cash received from individuals and ferries 1860-87; fines received at courts of complaints and police courts 1860-87, and other miscellaneous accounts 1860-87**
Disbursements and receipts on poor account 1875-1916.
Miscellaneous accounts (contd. From vol.3)** 1887-1910.

* Some duplication between vol.1 and 2 where dates overlap.
** Vol.3 and 5 indexed.

MS. 6397

Audits of half yearly company accounts and poor accounts. 1841-1908.

1. 1841-1859
2. 1860-1908*

* Includes repair accounts for Penge church.

MS. 6398

Court of binding and making free :- "day books" recording the names of apprentices bound and freemen admitted and fees paid at weekly court meetings. 1794-1924.

1. 1794-1827*
2. 1827-56**
3. 1857-81
4. 1881-1907

* Formerly MS. 6398A
** Formerly MS. 6398

MS. 6398A

Re-catalogued as MS. 6398/1.

MS. 6399

Alphabetical list of free watermen, giving their ages. 1827.

MS. 6400

Account books of payment to pensioners, arranged alphabetically within periods of about five years, giving ages (1809-33), addresses, dates of admission to or discharge from pension and stating when married or dead. 1794-1928.

1. 1794-1818
2. 1819-1838
3. 1839-1866
4. 1867-1890
5. 1891-1910

For earlier accounts see MS. 6395.

MS. 6401

Quarterage lodgers, giving addresses or moorings and stating when dead. 1804-1923.

1808-1859 A-L
1804-1859 N-Y
1859-1880 A-K
1859-1880 L-Y
4A. 1880-1903 A-K
1880-1903 L-Y
1901-1923 A-K
1901-1923 L-Y

Note: page reference are to register of freemen, MS. 6307.

Burton. James

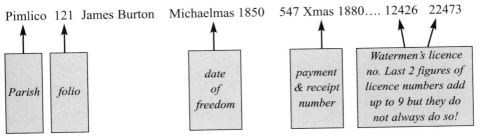

[Above information from Clerk of the Company of Watermen and Lightermen
Referring to records held at Guildhall, London.]

Key to information in Quarterage ledges, 1859 - 1923.
MS. 6401.

MS. 6402

Quarterage collection and account books, giving places of abode and accounts paid,
arranged under collectors' names. 1796-1917.

Vol.1.   1796*-1804
[Vol.2.   now MS. 6402A/1.]
Vol.3.   1805-1823
Vol.4.   1823-1842
Vol.5.   1841-1858
Vol.6.   1859-1868
Vol.7.   1869-1877
Vol.8.   1878-1886

Vol.9.   1887-1895
Vol.10.   1896-1905
Vol.11.   1905-17

* See MS. 6404 for 1785-1796.
Note: page reference up to Vol.8) and MS. 6307/1 (plain numerical references up to vol.8) and MS. 6307/2 ('N' reference up to vol.8 and plain numerical reference thereafter).

MS. 6402 A

Alphabetical list of masters, of apprentices giving addresses or moorings and dates of bindings and turning over with references to registers of apprentices bindings.* 1797-1938.

1. 1797-1852**
2. 1841-1852***
3. 1853-1938****

* MS. 6289
** Formerly MS. 6402/2. (letters A-O and S-Y only)
*** Some duplication with vol.1, letters A-B only
**** Formerly MS. 18,550.

MS. 6403

Lists of quarterage defaulters. 1843-1876.

Note: page references refer to registers of freemen, MS. 6307.

MS. 6404

Rough quarterage collection book* giving places of abode and amounts paid, arranged under collectors' names. 1785-1796.

See also MS. 6402 for quarterage collection 1796-1905.
* Begins at p.347.

MS. 6405

Index, ? to quarterage record no longer extant. c.1763-c.1794.

Note: a former inscription on the cover of this volume – 'widows' quarterage' – was misleading.

MS. 6406

Gravesend quarterage books, alphabetically arranged. c.1814-1929. Incomplete.

Vol.1. c.1814-1858
Vol.2. 1859-1883
Vol.3. c.1891-1929.

Note: page reference refer to registers of freemen, MS. 6307.

MS. 6407

Dinner bill book. 1801-1805.

MS. 6408

Register of steamboats, giving owners, numbers of permitted passengers, and masters' names and addresses, with index to boats and masters. 1846-1848.

MS. 6408 A

Measurement book of steamboats. 19th Cent.

MS. 6409

Beadle's time books 1843-1877, and Inspector's books 1877-1909 (incomplete), listing hours of attendance and activities of company offices.

1. 1843-53*
2. 1853-62*
3. 1863-66
4. 1867-70
5. 1870-73
6. 1874-77
7. 1877-80
8. 1880-82
9. 1882-84
10. 1884-88
11. 1888-94

12. 1895-6**
13. 1898-1904
14. 1905-9

* Hours of attendance only.
** Loose papers extracted from vol.11; probably rough drafts of missing volume.

MS. 6409A

Beadles' time and log books. 1828-1835

1. outdoor beadle's diary of daily official activities 1828-1830;
2. time keeping book recording (? House) beadle's attendance at hall and elsewhere 1828-1830;
3. outdoor beadle's (J. W. Hartley) diary of daily official activities 1828-1830;
4. diary of staff attendance at hall and appointments 1829-1830;
5. log book*, of J.E Outler London Bridge station, July-Sept. 1835;
6. log book of J.W Hartley, July 1835;
7. log book, West India docks station, with alphabetical list of steamboats, July-Sept. 1835.

* Gives account of passing traffic including names of boats and time past station.

MS. 6410

Register of plying places, indicating locations of marks (unfinished fair copy). 1828.

MS. 6410A

Rough register of plying places, indicating locations of marks, 1813, with notes of additional marks and marks examined to 1828. 1813-1828.

MS. 6411

Register of plying places, indicating locations of marks, with notes of annual examination of marks, 1887-1906. Commenced c. 1885.

MS. 6412

Book of plying places below London bridge:- north side. 1833-1886.

See also MS. 6329.

MS. 6413

Book of plying places above London bridge:- north side. 1833-1887.

MS. 6413A

Book of plying places, London bridge to Windsor. 1812.

MS. 6414

Book of legal opinions. 1730-1815.

MS. 6415

Stewards' half-yearly signed receipt book "for money to be paid to the poor watermen of the parishes St. Margaret and St. John, Westminster," as a recompense of the interest in Sunday ferries". 1750-1791.

MS. 6416

'Random' poor account, listing receipts for company poor box, mainly from courts of complaint and binding, and disbursements at these courts. 1811-1815.

MS. 6417

Company's general receipt books. 1793-1830.

Vol.1. 1793-1802
Vol.2. 1802-1830
Vol.3. 1803-1811

MS. 6596

Almshouse committee minute book, including entries relating to the building and establishment of the almshouses. 1838-1858.

For rough notes and minutes, 1841 see MS. 6821.

MS. 6597
Penge church committee minute book, relating to the construction of a church at Penge, near the company's almshouses. 1846-1853.

MS. 6598

Almshouses annual subscription books (lists of those subscribing with amount of annual subscription). 1840-1951.

1. 1840-84*
2. 1885-1922*
3. 1923-51**

* Alphabetical order.
** Chronological order.

MS. 6599

Almshouses journals. 1849-1922.

1. 1849-74
2. 1875-97
3. 1898-1922

MS. 6600

Cash books relating to the Asylums at Penge and Ditchling, and to the General benevolent fund. 1839-1942.

1. 1839-92.
2. 1885-1945
Some duplication of information where dates overlap.

MS. 6601

Almshouses ledger. 1839-1879.

MS. 6602

Books of payments to inmates of the almshouses. 1841-1859.

Vol.1. 1841-1842
Vol.2. 1843-1845
Vol.3. 1846-1848
Vol.4. 1849-1851

Vol.5. 1852-1855
Vol.6. 1855-1859

MS. 6819

Receivers' books of quarterage accounts, giving names, places of abode or moorings, and amounts paid. 1764-1767 and 1791-1793.

Vol.1. 1764-7, not signed.
Vol.2. 1791-3, signed.

MS. 6820

Comptrollers' book of quarterage accounts, giving places of abode or moorings, names, and amounts paid. 1791-1793.

MS. 6821

Almshouses committee rough minute book. 1841.
See also MS. 6596.

MS. 6822

Weavers Company

Three deeds and two receipts relating to company property, i.e. one messuage with appurtenances formerly called "The Boar's head", then known by the name and sign of "The horse shoe", situate in Bread St. in the parish of Allhallows Bread Street. 1661 (2 items), and 1668 (3 items).

MS. 6823

A collection of deeds, briefs, reports and other legal documents relating to property situate in the parish of St. Michael, Cornhill. 1770-1922. 34 items in 2 bundles.

Bundle 1.   Papers relating to the case of Buller v. Vincent 1782/3.
            Schedule attached.
Bundle 2.   Title deeds, etc. 1770-1922.
(Ex. Hertfordshire County Record Office:- Dimsdale collection).

MS. 8910

Book of copies of protections for company officials, their servants and ferrymen protected from the impress, giving ages, physical descriptions and addresses of watermen. 1803-10.

MS. 8911

Alphabetical list of watermen in HM Navy with names of the ships on which they were serving ("when last heard of by their relatives"). 1803-09.

MS. 9075

Inventory of furniture and fixtures at company's hall. September, 1849.

MS. 9923

Bank account book. (The company in account with the Bank of England). 1828-1860. Latter half blank.

MS. 10021

Court of binding and making free:- comptroller's signed account book, giving places of abode and amounts paid. 1825-1827

See also MS. 6297/4, 6298/4-5..

MS. 10022

Register of boats for hire, numerically arranged, giving names and abodes or moorings of watermen or craft owner, and names and types of boats. 1827-1859. Indexed

MS. 10799

Papers:- correspondence with Admiralty relating to impressment and a list of watermen eligible for service to be drawn up in 1855; report of management committee of asylums (1855); report of improvement committee (1856); clerk's analysis of persons holding woodmongers' numbers and their number of craft (1855); papers relating to members' privileges; and report on the duties of the 3 beadles and the appointment of a new solicitor. 1855-1858.

MS. 14924

Register of watermen, recording addresses. Incomplete; c.100 names.
Indexed in MS. 14925. 1827.

MS. 14925

Index of members names in MS. 14924. 1827.

MS. 14926

Account of fines received by the clerk, 1827-42, with account of extra quarterage* paid for posts, piles and tables of rates, 1829-42.

* For detailed account of extra quarterage, 1829-31, see MS. 14928.

MS. 14927

Account book of purchase and disbursement of freedom and indenture stamps. 1793-1810. Audited.

MS. 14928

Account book: detailed accounts of extra quarterage paid by Hallam and Cutler, 1829-31.

1 vol, most pages cut out.

See accounts of extra quarterage in MS. 14926.
See also MS. 14930.

MS. 14929

Receipt book of salaries. 1884-1909.

1. 1884-87
2. 1897-1909.

MS. 14930

Loose papers found in MS. 14928:- rough lists of asylum subscriptions (for the company's almshouses at Penge, Kent), 1866-75; summons to Henry Hines for navigating after his licence had expired, 1877; draft petition to the Thames Navigation

Committee of the Port of London to reject application of steam ferry company to erect pontoons, undated; and blank forms notifying expiry of licence. c.1866-77.

MS. 18631

Polling papers (blank) for the almshouses at Penge, Surrey, listing candidates with ages, addresses, and details of their work on the river. 1922, 1927, 1929, 1932, 1934 and 1956. Printed in folder, in box.

MS. 18632

Blank forms of application for licences; blank certificates and licences for apprentices, freemen, and the use of various types of boat; application forms and stock letters re Penge almshouses applications; and summons forms etc. re complaints and misdemeanours. 19th-20th.cent.

Paper and Parchment, printed 33 items in folder, in box.

MS.18633

Notices, etc. issued by the company including petitions to the House of Commons re steam boat accidents (with list of accidents 1835-6), the Steam Vessels (Thames) bill, and the Gravesend pier bill; scale (i.e. Measurements) for wherries and skiffs; and duties of the outdoor and hall beadles and order of Lord Major's day processions. 19th-20th.cent.

Paper printed 11 items in envelope, in box.

MS. 18634

Court lists, 1855-91, giving names and addresses of court members.

Paper, 6sh, in envelope, in box.

MS. 19546

Alphabetical list of apprentices bound, giving data of binding and address, with name and address of master, 1833-44.

Called 'Master's and Apprentices' addresses'.

MS. 19547

Apprentice's licence number book. 1908-1920.

MS. 19548

Alphabetical list of barge owners with addresses. Undated, early 20th cent.

MS. 19548 A

'Register of contracts'- list of men contracted (i.e., articled) to Master watermen or lightermen, with date of grant of licence by the company where applicable. 1865-1926. Indexed

Note: under s.53ff. of the Thames Conservancy Act 1854 (27-8 Vict. c.113) men too old to serve an apprenticeship could serve a 2-year 'contract' to a Master watermen or lightermen, and if found satisfactory obtain a licence from the watermen's company.

MS. 19549

Ledger of money owed by members to the Company for meals, refreshments, playing cards etc. 1807-12.

MS. 19550 > Now catalogued at MS. 6402 A/3.

'The privilege book' 1853-1933.

MS. 19551

Account book relating to Ditchling almshouses. 1897-1914.
Mainly blank.

MS. 19552

Record of rent paid by tenants of property in Penge and at 19 St Mary at Hill. 1849-52.

MS. 19553

Penge rents ledger. 1949-71.

MS. 19554

Asylums ledgers. 1884-1918.

1884-1911
1912-1918

MS. 19555

Asylums rough cash book* 1893-1917.

Mainly Blank.

* For fair copy see MS6600.

MS. 19556

Almshouses donations books, recording names and amounts of donations, with some addresses.

1. 1839-1864
2. 1865-1920

MS. 19557

Westminster Sunday Ferry charity:- book of receipts and expenditure. 1886-1951.

MS. 22359

Register of licences granted to men at the end of their contract (i.e. articles) to a Master watermen or lightermen, in licence number order, giving man's name; master's name and (to 1911) district; date of contract; date of licence; also (to 1911) to folio reference in the register of contracts (now MS. 19548A), and the date of (?) approval of the licence by the court of company. 1886-1971.

(Entries 1-309 missing)
For 'contracts' see the note to MS. 19548A.

MS. 22360

Birth register of contract men':- register of men contracted (i.e. articled) to serve a Master watermen or lightermen, giving dates and place of birth and baptism, arranged in date order of contracts. 1865-1923.

For 'contracts' see the note to MS. 19548A.

MS. 22361

Contract rough book' recording names and addresses of men contracted (i.e. articled) and of their masters, and also names and addresses of men applying for licences from the company at the end of their contracts (articles), and of application of licence. 1865-1910.

For fair copy record see MS. 199548A.
For 'contracts' see the note to MS. 19548A.

Transcribed by Talisa Legon, compiled by James W. Legon. Details correct as at October 2007

Appendix XI 1671 Table of fares

	Oar		Skuller	
	s.	d.	s.	d.
From London to Limehouse, New Crane, Shadwell Dock, Bell Wharfe, Ratclift Cross	1	0	0	6
To Wapping Dock, Wapping New and Wapping Old Stairs, the Hermitage, Rotherhith Church Stairs and Rotherhith Stairs	0	6	0	3
From St Olave's to Rotherhith Church Stairs and Rotherhith Stairs	0	6	0	3
From Billingsgate and St Olave's to St Saviour's Mill	0	6	0	3
All The Stairs between London Bridge and Westminster	0	6	0	3
From either side above London Bridge, to Lambeth And Fox-hall	1	0	0	6
From Whitehall to Lambeth and Fox-hall	0	6	0	3
From Temple, Dorset, Blackfryers Stairs, and Paul's Wharf, to Lambeth	0	8	0	4
Over the water directly, (for the next sculler) between London Bridge and Limehouse, or London Bridge And Fox-hall	..		0	2

Oars	Whole Fare		Company	
	s.	d.	s.	d.
From London to Gravesend	4	6	0	9
From London to Grayes or Greenhive	4	0	0	8
From London to Purfleet or Eriff	3	0	0	6
From London to Woolwich	2	6	0	4
From London to Blackwall	2	0	0	4
From London to Greenwich or Debtford	1	6	0	3
From London to Chelsey, Battersey, or Wandsworth	1	6	0	3
From London to Putney, Fulham, or Barn Elms	2	0	0	4
From London to Hammersmith, Chiswick, or Mortlack	2	6	0	6
From London to Brentford. Isleworth, Richmond	3	6	0	6

From London to Twickenham	4	0	0	6
From London to Kingstone	5	0	0	9
From London to Hampton Court	6	0	1	0
From London to Hampton Town, Sunbury, and Walton-upon Thames	7	0	1	0
From London to Weybridge and Chertsey	10	0	1	0
From London to Stanes	12	0	1	6
From London to Windsor	14	0	2	0

Rates for carrying of Goods in the Tilt-boat between Gravesend and London

	s.	d.
A half ffirkine	0	1
Whole ffirkine	0	2
Hogshead	2	0
100 weight of cheese, iron, or any other such heavy goods	0	4
Sack of salt or corn	0	6
An ordinary chest or trunk	0	6
An ordinary hamper	0	6
The hire of the whole Tilt-boat when one or more persons have occasion to hire it themselves	22	6
Every single person in the ordinary passage	0	6

Source: History of the Waterman's Company, by Henry Humpherus

Appendix XII Numbers of apprentices by year

Year	Count		Year	Count
1674	454		1763	281
1675	344		1764	254
1676	263		1765	218
1677	315		1766	244
1678	382		1767	213
1679	469		1768	230
1680	452		1769	214
1681	377		1770	220
1682	423		1771	266
1683	339		1772	260
1684	375		1773	206
1685	378		1774	215
1686	388		1775	221
1687	444		1776	246
1688	393		1777	222
1689	520		1778	237
1690	427		1779	251
1691	532		1780	257
1692	484		1781	263
1693	493		1782	270
1694	545		1783	318
1695	527		1784	270
1696	438		1785	232
1697	542		1786	242
1698	333		1787	220
1699	283		1788	226
1750	260		1789	236
1751	201		1790	192
1752	210		1791	234
1753	193		1792	195
1754	191		1793	233
1755	259		1794	209
1756	246		1795	259
1757	290		1796	281
1758	248		1797	274
1759	247		1798	272
1760	244		1799	276
1761	253		1850	269
1762	248		1851	256

1852	230	1867	389 (12)
1853	277	1868	344 (8)
1854	337	1869	389 (20)
1855	339	1870	274 (12)
1856	312	1871	371 (16)
1857	331	1872	337 (23)
1858	314	1873	337 (33)
1859	254	1874	356 (22)
1860	387	1875	395 (23)
1861	426	1876	333 (25)
1862	381	1877	360 (25)
1863	421	1878	355 (35)
1864	341	1879	272 (16)
1865	366 (48)	1880	261 (17)
1866	417 (23)	1881	214 (15)

Source: History of the Waterman's Company, by Henry Humpherus.

It can be seen that the years 1700-1749 and 1800-1849, are missing, although Humpherus asserts that they are previously recorded. I can find no reference to these numbers throughout his works.

Prior to these years Humpherus asserts that between 15th October 1656 and 28th June 1665 there were 2912 apprentices bound. He further asserts that the register book from June 1665 to November 1673 was lost.

It is interesting to note that as he quotes, presumably from having seen the register, the numbers between 1674 and 1692, this register, which he must have seen sometime after his appointment in 1849, has now too been lost. The numbers cannot therefore be verified.

Numbers of Freedoms granted by year 1766-1849

Year	Number	Year	Number
1766	164	1805	140
1767	136	1806	136
1768	145	1807	161
1769	147	1808	171
1770	138	1809	193
1771	125	1810	179
1772	129	1811	215
1773	125	1812	142
1774	105	1813	164
1775	113	1814	238
1776	194	1815	265
1777	123	1816	214
1778	94	1817	210
1779	88	1818	253
1780	95	1819	201
1781	107	1820	186
1782	107	1821	180
1783	100	1822	237
1784	192	1823	181
1785	170	1824	149
1786	170	1825	165
1787	158	1826	169
1788	154	1827	214
1789	168	1828	197
1790	230	1829	203
1791	228	1830	158
1792	229	1831	161
1793	115	1832	164
1794	100	1833	164
1795	101	1834	159
1796	172	1835	171
1797	152	1836	144
1798	139	1837	143
1799	276	1838	146
1800	153	1839	169
1801	161	1840	152
1802	330	1841	164
1803	184	1842	230
1804	163	1843	199

844	175	1847	155
845	136	1848	161
846	179	1849	228

ource: History of the Waterman's Company, by Henry Humpherus.

.ppendix XIII A list of the members of the Company of Lightermen and Vatermen, with their several avocations in 1809.

erving in His Majesty's navy, in person, or by substitute .s per list A	518
.t sea and supposed to be chiefly in His Majesty's service, r in French prisons, or have lost their lives during the war, .s per list B	266
illed, wounded, or invalided during the war*	105
ı the service of the Board of Customs, as Established, referable, and Extra Watermen	290
•itto Excise	45
rotected by and employed by the Board of Ordnance at ravesend	125
y ditto at the Tower and Woolwich	52
argemen and Artillery at Woolwich	16
ıpress service at Gravesend	44
itto at London	14
owns and River Pilots	68
is Majesty's Bargemen and Watermen, and 'atermen Pensioners	50
argemen to the Lords Commissioners of the Admiralty	18
itto Treasurer of the Navy	17
argemen of the Lords Commissioners of the Navy	29
itto Commissioners of the Victualling Office	12
itto of the Board of Green Cloth	10
itto in the service of the Transport Board	9
the service at His Majesty's Dockyard, Deptford	9
the service of the Elder Brethren of the Trinity House	10
the service and protected by the East India Company	21
the service of the London Dock Company	5
itto West India Dock Company	4

Protected by the Master of His Majesty's Mint	4
Ditto by the Herald's Office	2
Ditto and employed by the General Post Office	3
Employed by the Marshal of the Admiralty Court	4
Bargemen of the Right Honourable the Lord Mayor, the Water Bailiff and Committee of Thames Navigation	47
In the employment of the Superintendent of the city canal	4
In the service and employ of the police magistrates for the county of Middlesex	37
In the employ of the respective Fire Offices	459
Protected and employed by the Company of Watermen and Lightermen	22
Masters and Owners of craft, many of them Liverymen of the City of London	291
Sailing Masters of Sloops, Lighters, and Barges, sailing under Custom House Registers	147
Liverymen of the City of London	88
Licensed Victuallers	22
Fellowship Porters, and Corn and Coal Meters	38
Officers and Privates of the several Marine Volunteers Corps, on the river Thames, many of whom are masters and owners of craft, and a great portion of them apprentices	1,020
Watermen protected by Peers of the Realm	7
Apprentices who have not served fours years about	900
Aged, Decayed and Infirm Watermen and Lightermen about	300
(Description omitted in copy)	191
	5,323

*See Appendix IX

Source: History of the Waterman's Company, by Henry Humpherus

Appendix XIV London's Docks

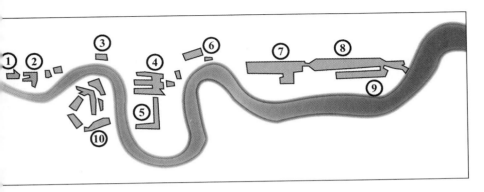

21. London Docks sketch map

1. St Katherine Dock 1828-1969

The St Katharine Docks, which are situated to the east of Tower Bridge, were the closest docks to the City of London. They were built on the site of the former church of St Katherine's, (a plaque commemorates this). 11,300 people were displaced, with 1250 houses and tenements pulled down. St Katharine's, designed by Thomas Telford, comprised two connected basins, the east dock and the west dock. The docks were linked to the river through an entrance lock, nearly 200 feet in length, fitted with three pairs of gates. The wet docks comprised nearly 12 acres. Warehouses, six storeys high and supported by heavy Tuscan columns, were built on the quayside so that cargo could be unloaded directly from ships into the storerooms. The warehouses were up to 500 feet long and up to 165 feet deep. St Katharine's Docks were used mainly for valuable cargoes, such as ivory, shells, sugar, marble, rubber, carpets, spices and perfumes. Many of these cargoes were brought in by barge from the lower docks. The docks have now been redeveloped for leisure and residential use.

2. London Docks 1805-1968

The London Docks are situated about half a mile downriver from St Katharine Docks at Wapping. Opened in 1805, the entrance to the dock was from the Thames at Shadwell. The facilities at Wapping took up an area of nearly 90 acres, of which 35 acres consisted of water, and there were almost 2.5 miles of quay and jetty frontage. The docks were surrounded by a high wall and had room for more than 300 vessels. The warehouses, four storeys high, had space for over 200,000 tons of goods. The dock was used by short-sea traders, carrying cargoes such as tobacco, dried fruit, canned goods, ivory, wool and spices.

3. Regents Canal Dock 1820-1969

East of the London Docks lay the Regent's Canal Dock, designed by John Nash, at Limehouse, of about 10 acres. Opened in 1820, it connected Regent's Canal with the Thames. It is now known as Limehouse Marina. This dock was one of the first to use hydraulic power. A small pumping station was built on the west side of the Commercial Road locks. A steam engine was used to pump water into a system of mains that supplied the cranes and other hydraulic machinery. A basin was also built where canal boats could wait for the right state of the tide before passing through the locks.

4. West India Docks 1802/06-1980

On the Isle of Dogs, to the east of London Docks, lay the West India Docks, designed by William Jessop. The site comprised an import dock of 30 acres of water and an export dock of about 24 acres. Together, they had space for more than 600 large ships. At each end of the docks was a basin connecting them to the river, with locks to control the flow of water between the docks and the Thames. Locks were also constructed in the cuts joining the docks with the basins. Ships entered on the Blackwall side of the basin and the lighters went in at the Limehouse end. Five-storey warehouses were also built.

Whilst initially built for the West India trade, the docks later handled general cargoes. South of the import and export docks was the South Dock, which was opened in 1870 (formerly the City Canal, built so that vessels could avoid sailing around the Isle o Dogs). The West India Docks have now been transformed, and are dominated by the huge towers of Canary Wharf .

5. Millwall Docks 1868-1980

The Millwall Docks, situated on the Isle of Dogs to the south of the West & East India Docks, dealt mainly in grain and timber, from the Baltic. The dock area was dominated by the Central Granary, which occupied the north-western corner, and its associated pneumatic grain elevators. By the 1920s, Millwall Docks had been linked with the West India Docks by new cuttings. At that time the docks contained 160 acres of water and seven miles of working quaysides. The facilities were further upgraded in the 1950s and 60s.

6. East India Docks 1806-1967

Eastwards, downriver, of the West India Docks were the East India Docks. Opened in 1806, the docks originally served the East India Company's trading interests in India nd other parts of Asia. The docks consisted of parallel import and export docks with a basin and locks connecting to the river. In later years, the 31 acres of water at the docks, were used by ships such as those from the Ellerman Line, Union Castle Line and Blue Star. In the 1920s, new facilities were built for the handling of frozen meat. The export lock was badly bombed during the Second World War and filled-in.

The Royal Docks:

The Royal Docks, at the time the most modern of their kind, formed the largest area of dock space in the world. Although now empty and deserted, (save for London City airport in their midst), they are still an awe inspiring sight. They comprised:

7. Royal Victoria 1855-1980

Opened by Prince Albert in 1855, the Royal Victoria Dock was built slightly to the east of the mouth of the River Lea and covers almost 100 acres of water, incorporating several new features.

Five finger-jetties projected into the dock from the main quays, to aid quick delivery of cargoes, after sorting into barges on the opposite side of the jetty to which the ship was berthed. There was also a tidal basin at the western end, with ships entering the basin via a lock from the Thames.

The Dock was also the first in London to be directly connected with the national railway system, which allowed imported goods to be moved around the country much faster than before. The dock was also the first to be equipped with hydraulic machinery and lifts to raise ships. The dock was extensively rebuilt in the late 1930s and closed to commercial shipping in the early 1980s.

8. Royal Albert 1880-1980

To the east of the Victoria Docks is the Royal Albert Dock, at the time it was opened it was the largest dock in the world. It was designed to take ocean-going vessels of up to 12,000 tons. At 1.75 miles, it is staggeringly long. It contained more than 16,500 feet of deep-water quays. It was connected to the Royal Victoria Dock by a lock. The entrance to the dock was via a large lock and basin at Gallions Reach. There were single storey transit sheds rather than warehouses, to emphasise the fast turn around for ships. It was also the first London dock to be lit by electricity. The main cargoes handled at the Royal Albert Dock were tobacco, chilled and frozen meat, grain and general cargo.

9. King George V 1921-1983

To the south of the Royal Albert Dock was the King George V Dock, (known simply a KGV). It was the last of the docks to be completed, in 1921, and is over 4000 feet, with nearly 3 miles of quays. The entrance lock from the river, the largest in the Port o London, was 800 feet long and 100 feet wide. Through it passed the ships of the Blue Star Line, British India Steam Navigation Company, Albion Line and P&O group Ships of up to 30,000 tons could be accommodated in the dock. The largest ship ever to use it was the 35,000-ton RMS Mauretania in 1939, which narrowly squeezed in.

10. Surrey Commercial Docks (incorporating the Greenland Dock and Easter Country Dock) 1807-1969

The Surrey Docks were the only docks situated on the south side of the river, opposite Limehouse. The Commercial Dock Company had purchased the Greenland Dock a Rotherhithe in 1807. It was used for the North European trade in timber, hemp, iron, ta and corn. The company eventually owned all the docks built at Rotherhithe over the following 70 years. The interconnected complex of docks, basins, timber ponds and waterways of the Surrey complex extended for over 150 acres of water, and were surrounded by nearly five miles of quayside. Apart from the Greenland Dock and Eas Country Dock, in which general cargo from many countries was unloaded, they were devoted to the handling and storage of timber.

Appendix XV Subscriptions of the Court for the building of the first asylum

	£.	s.
Master		
Mr John Drew	10	10
Senior Warden		
Mr James J. Thompson	21	0
Junior Wardens		
Mr William Bradley	10	10
Mr Thomas Hill	5	5
Mr John Cracklow	5	5
Assistants		
Mr John Drinkwald	105	0
Mr Robert Thompson	21	0
Mr Joseph Turnley	21	0
Mr Robert Banyon	10	10
Mr William Randall	5	5
Mr Charles Hay	31	10
Mr Charles T. White	10	10
Mr Francis Flower	5	5
Mr James Thomas	10	10
Mr E.P. Sells	10	10
Mr John Raymond	10	10
Mr John Dudin Brown	52	10
Mr Thomas Young	105	0
Mr William H. Hobbs	10	10
Mr John Addis	52	10
Mr Robert Goulding	52	10
Mr James William Turnley	10	10
Mr Thomas Groves	26	5
Mr Richard Robbins	10	10
Mr Charles Francis	10	10
Hon. Secs. And Solicitors		
Messrs. Clark, Straight & Cooper	21	0
Clerk [to the Company]		
Mr John Banyon	10	10

Source: History & Origin by Henry Humpherus

Appendix XVI 1628/29 Admiralty Muster of Watermen

Nicholas Abbott
Robert Abram
John Acombe
Nathaniell Actin
John Addames
John Addams
John Addams
John Addams
Thomas Addams
John Addams
Thomas Addison
Thomas Addison
John Adee
William Agde
Thomas Agood
Mathew Alderidge
Richard Alebury
David Aleway
William Alixander
Richard Allan
Griffin Allen
John Allen
John Allom
Symon Allowe
William Allyn
Richard Allyne
John Allyson
Miles Almound
Ffrancis Aloright
John Amor
John Andrew
Thomas Andrewes
William Andrewes
Oliver Andrewes
Edward Andrewes
Robert Andrewes
Robert Andrews
Richard Angell
William Ansell

Jeffery Ansell
Henry Ansell
Robert Ansell
William Anthonie
Richard Anthony
Richard Anthony
John Ap Evans
Evan ap Proctor
Mathew Arden
Thomas Arnold
Rogger Arnold
William Arnold
Richard Arnold
Thomas Arnold
Richard Arnold
Thomas Arnold
John Arnold
Robert Arnold
John Arnold
Edward Arnold
Henry Arnott
Ralph Arrowsmith
Robert Arther
Edward Arthur
Nicholas Arthur
James Arthur
Robert Arthur
George Ashby
Thomas Ashes
James Ashley
Thomas Ashwell
John Ashwell
William Askewe
William Askewe
Walter Aston
Thomas Atkins
Ffrancis Atkinson
Thomas Atkinson
William Atterbury

John Attwell
Giles Austine
Edward Averell
George Axe
William Axe
Abraham Aylett
Robert Aymon
Adrian Ayres
Thomas Ayres
Thomas Ayres
John Bacon
John Bailie
Thomas Baker
Alexsander Baker
John Baker
Nicholas Balch
William Balden
Mathias Ballard
Michaiell Ballard
John Banneston
Edward Barker
William Barnes
Alexander Barnes
Edward Barratt
John Barrell
George Barren
John Barres
Richard Barrett
John Barrett
Gregory Barrett
William Barrowes
Thomas Bartermen
Thomas Bartholmew
Thomas Bartholmew
Thomas Bartlet
John Bartlett
Ffrancis Bartlett
Andrew Bartlett
John Bash
Thomas Bash
Edward Baskervill

Anthony Bason
John Bason
Gregory Bastable
Abraham Bate[Illegible]
Jonathan Bateman
John Bateman
Henry Bayley
William Bayly
Charelle Beach
Michaiell Beadwell
William Beasley
Henry Beast
John Beavis
John Bechworth
George Becke
Ralph Beckham
John Beckley
Tristeram Beddoe
John Bedfeild
Steeven Bedford
William Bedford
Christopher Beech
Yeoman Bell
Thomas Bellinger
John Belson
Jonas Benn
William Bennet
Rogger Bennett
John Benton
Robert Betts
William Bevan
William Biby
Robert Bickerstafe
Steephen Bidgood
Henry Biggeland
John Biggs
John Billingdore
Henry Bilsby
Edward Bingham
Thomas Bird
Henry Birke

John Bishope
John Bishopp
John Bishoppe
John Black
Roger Blacke
William Blackewell
Thomas Blakeman
Henry Blaney
Robert Blanke
John Blany
Thomas Bleake
George Blewe
Ralph Blower
Ralph Blundell
William Board
William Board
Henry Boddy
Robert Boddy
Richard Boddy
George Boddy
Lawrence Bodicinn
Thomas Bolderstone
Clement Bolton
William Bomfourd
Richard Bonnd
Batholmew Bonnd
Peeter Bonnocke
Nathaniell Bonnocke
John Bonnocke
William Bonnocke
George Bonnocke
George Bonns
Edward Booth
Phillipe Booth
Richard Bostone
William Bosworth
Richard Boulton
Robert Bound
Edward Bourne
Abraham Bourne
John Bower

Thomas Bowers
Thomas Bowes
Nicholas Bowes
Henry Bowles
John Bowman
Anthony Bowman
William Boyce
John Boyer
Richard Boyer
Thomas Brackenbury
Robert Bradmore
John Brafferton
John Braggington
John Brasington
Ffrancis Bray
John Bray
Arthur Bray
Thomas Bray
John Brewer
John Brewer
Edward Brewer
John Brewis
John Brice
William Brice
Thomas Brickland
Ffrancis Brierly
William Brimskine
Richard Brisby
Joseph Broad
Richard Broad
Jeromie Broadbacke
John Broade
James Brocke
John Brocke
Peeter Brooke
Robert Browell
William Brown
Samuell Browne
Henry Browne
John Browne
Obediah Browne

Thomas Browne
Thomas Browne
Jehosaphat Browne
Robert Browne
Thomas Browne
Peeter Browne
John Browne
Thomas Browne
Robert Browne
Henry Browne
Brobert Browne
Abraham Browne
James Browne
John Browne
Ralph Browne
Robert Browne
Thomas Browne
Ambrose Browne
Robert Browne
Thomas Browne
Anthony Browne
Thomas Browne
John Browne
Thomas Browne
William Browne
Edward Browne
Joseph Browne
Thomas Browne
William Browne
Audrian Browneman
Richard Browninge
Richard Bruninge
Robert Bryan
John Bryan
William Bryan
Robert Bryan
John Bryant
John Bucke
George Buckingham
Charles Buckland
Edward Buckland

Richard Buckland
Rowland Buckland
Thomas Bugbey
Walter Bugge
Guy Bullock
William Bunniford
John Burch
Randall Burd
John Burges
Thomas Burges
William Burley
Edward Burley
Nathaniell Burly
Thomas Burnam
John Burnam
Thomas Burnham
Robbert Burr
George Burridge
Mathew Burrowes
Richard Burrowes
Robert Bursey
Robt Burton
Oswell Burtone
William Busby
James Bushwood
Richard Buske
Rogger Butcher
Thomas Butcher
John Butcher
Xpopher Butler
Xpopher Buttler
Hugh Byby
John Byby
Robert Byby
William Byby
Edmond Bycrofte
Thomas Cable
Richard Cable
George Callopnie
Thomas Callowhill
John Callowhill

Ffrancis Calvert
Oliver Camminge
Thomas Cane
William Canner
Robt Cannocke
Robert Cannon
John Cannon
John Careles
Robert Careles
Xpopher Careles
Christopher Carelesse
William Carey
Samuell Carpenter
Henry Carpenter
John Carpenter
[Illegible] Carson
George Carter
William Carter
John Carter
John Carter
John Carter
Robert Cas
Trusteram Case
Rogger Casier
Edmonnd Catleford
Richard Catt[Illegible]
Edward Catterill
Symonnd Cave
John Cawley
Robert Celarke
William Chamberline
Hugh Chamberowe
Edmond Chambers
Edmond Chambers
John Chamblaine
Nicholas Chandler
Nicholas Chandler
George Channt
Thomas Chapell
Walter Chapell
James Chapman

Henry Chapman
Henry Chappel
John Chappell
William Chappell
Ffrancis Charelesworth
Nicholas Charte
David Chassmore
Thomas Chayre
William Cheeseman
Gyles Childerston
William Chippley
Reynold Chittingtone
Richard Chiveley
Richard Choyett
James Christian
John Christian
Robert Christian
Thomas Church
Josuah Church
Thomas Church
John Church
John Church
William Clarke
Thomas Clarke
John Clarke
Richard Clarke
Samuell Clarke
Walter Clarke
Richard Clarke
Leonard Clarke
William Clarke
John Clarke
Roger Clarke
Robert Clarke
Robert Clarke
Richard Clayton
John Cleare
William Clearke
Richard Clearke
William Clearke
John Clearke

obert Clearke
Thomas Clements
Adam Cleoke
ohn Clerke
ohn Clerke
ohn Clerke
ohn Clerke
Richard Clerke
John Clerke
William Clerke
Richard Cleven
John Cleyton
Thomas Clife
Edward Cliftone
John Clode
Thomas Clone
James Coale
Ralph Coales
Henry Coales
Ffrancis Cocke
Gregory Coe
Leonard Coe
Thomas Coke
Thomas Cole
Xpopher Cole
William Cole
Robert Coles
Allixander Collier
William Collins
Richard Collins
John Collins
Rowland Collyngrudge
William Colson
John Colson
Robert Combes
William Combes
Robert Combes
William Combes
John Combes
James Comer
Henry Comer

David Comes
Thomas Comminges
Andrew Compton
William Connon
James Connoway
Lawrence Connsell
Edward Conoway
Henry Consett
Robert Consett
Thomas Consett
William Consett
Thomas Consett
Thomas Consett
Walter Constant
Edward Conway
Xpopher Conyer
Richard Cooke
William Cooke
Richard Cooke
John Cooke
Thomas Cooke
Robert Cooke
Henry Coop
James Cooper
Ralph Cooper
Thomas Cooper
John Cooper
George Cooperthwart
Richard Cooter
William Copley
Samuell Corbett
Robert Corner
Xpopher Corner
Thomas Cory
Henry Cossens
Emanuell Coster
Thomas Coster
Abraham Cotterill
John Cotterill
John Cotterill
Anthony Cotterill

Phillipp Cotterill
Edward Cotterill
Thomas Cotterill
Robert Cotton
John Coulson
William Coulson
George Cousine
Deavoroux Cousine
Robert Cousins
George Cousins
Stephen Cousins
John Cowley
Richard Cox
Ffrancis Cox
Ffrancis Cox
John Cox
Henry Cox
John Cox
Thomas Cox
Anthony Cox
Peeter Coxfoote
Richard Cra[???]dge
Edward Cra[Illegible]
Thomas Cradocke
William Cragg
Thomas Cramp
William Cranaway
Henry Cranaway
Ffrancis Cranaway
William Crane
William Cressey
Daniell Crewe
John Crichman
John Cripps
Walter Cripps
Leonard Crispine
John Crispine
Henry Croft
John Crooke
Symon Croson
William Crosse

Thomas Crosse
James Crowdye
Martyne Crowley
Daniell Crumpe
John Curtis
John Curtis
Symonn Cutbert
Andrew Cutler
John Cutler
Edward Cuton
Richard Cuton
William Dalley
Hugh Dam[?]
Thomas Danghan
John Daniell
John Daniell
Nicholas Daniell
Robert Daniell
Edward Danngerfeild
William Danton
Abraham Darkine
Giles Dausey
William Davie
Daniell Davie
John Davies
Ellis Davies
Alixsander Davis
Ffrancis Davis
Richard Davis
John Davis
John Davis
John Davis
Evans Davis
Rice Davis
Richard Davis
Humfery Davis
Rogger Davis
Jeromie Davis
Owin Davis
William Davis
John Davis

Symon Davis
John Davis
Robert Dawes
Rogger Dawes
Richard Dawson
Anthonie Dawson
Robert Dawsone
William Daye
Richard Deane
Henry Deane
Richard Deane
Richard Deane
Anthonie Deane
John Deareinge
Henry Deerelove
Charelle Deerelove
Grifeth Denby
Thomas Dendye
James Denham
Richard Denny
John Derme
James Dernain
John Devill
Thomas Devin
John Dickeson
Richard Dickinson
John Dickinson
Robert Diggwood
William Dilkes
Nicholas Do[Illegible]
Richard Doane
John Doane
John Dobson
Steephen Dodd
Mathew Dodson
William Dodsone
Richard Dolye
William Dony
John Dotterill
James Douglas
Thomas Downsam

William Downsam
Walter Dowsey
Thomas Dowsey
John Dowsinge
Thomas Dowsinge
Anthonie Drake
John Draper
John Draper
William Drewett
Tobias Drine
John Driver
Thomas Driver
Thomas Driver
George Duby
Edward Duby
Thomas Duby
Richard Dudley
Richard Dunestone
Robert Duninge
Thomas Dunn
Richard Dupper
Richard Durseer
Thomas Dussell
Richard Dutton
Hugh Dutton
Rogger Dutton
William Dwite
Thomas Dwyte
John Dyer
William Dyer
Rogger Dyer
William Dynes
William Dynes
Andrew E[Illegible]
John Eagles
John Eaglestone
Anthonie Earle
Thomas Earle
John Earley
Robert Earlye
Thomas Easeman

John East
Robert East
Thomas East
Thomas Eastman
William Eaton
William Ebbes
William Ebbs
Steephen Echell
Robert Edge
John Edge
John Edge
John Edge
William Edmonnds
Thomas Edwarde
John Edwards
Stephen Edwards
William Edwards
Anthony Edwards
Thomas Edwin
John Eedes
Thomas Eedes
Thomas Elderwell
John Eldree
Symon Ellery
Robert Elliot
Robert Elliot
Richard Ellis
Thomas Ellis
Anthony Ellis
John Ellis
Robert Ellis
John Ellis
Richard Elton
Henry Elton
Richard Elvey
Ralph Emery
William Enfeild
John Etherintone
John Etherintone
James Evans
Richard Evans

William Evans
Nathaniell Evans
Oliver Evans
David Evans
Thomas Evans
Allixander Evans
Thomas Evans
Ffrancis Evans
John Evans
Richard Evans
John Evans
Nicholas Evans
Thomas Evans
Thomas Evans
Thomas Evans
John Evans
Richard Evans
William Evans
Thomas Evans
Hugh Evans
William Evans
Aryon Evans
William Evans
John Ewell
Ralph Ewer
John Eyres
John Eyres
Rogger Ff[Illegible]
William Ffare
David Ffarlonge
Robert Ffarmer
Robert Ffarthinge
Abraham Ffarwell
Thomas Ffease
Samuell Ffeild
Christopher Ffeildhowse
George Ffen
John Ffensenn
Luke Ffervall
Alixsander Ffettieplace
Robert Ffewell

Thomas Ffewell
Daniell Ffilkes
John Ffillcocke
David Ffinsburow
David Ffinsbury
Henry Ffireman
John Ffisher
John Ffisher
Rogger Ffisher
Joseph Fflanell
Hobby Fflavel
Nicholas Fflavel
Edward Ffleminge
Phillipe Ffleminge
George Ffleminge
John Ffleminge
Robert Ffletcher
John Ffletcher
Walter Fflewellinge
John Fflewinge
Martyne Fflinger
Henry Ffludd
Nicholas Ffludd
Abell Ffludd
Nicholas Ffludd
Phillippe Ffludd
Thomas Ffludd
Rowland Ffludd
Samuell Ffludd
Thomas Ffludd
Hugh Ffo[Illegible]
William Ffoggett
Richard Ffoote
Richard Fford
Ffrancis Fforeshippe
Richard Fforra
John Fforsett
John Ffosse
John Ffossett
William Ffossett
Hugh Ffoster

Lawrence Ffoster
John Ffoster
Samuell Ffoster
Richard Ffoster
Arthur Ffoster
William Ffoster
Henry Ffoulke
William Ffourd
Robert Ffowell
Peeter Ffowkes
William Ffowler
William Ffowler
Phillipe Ffowler
Henry Ffox
Edward Ffoxall
William Ffrain
Robert Ffrance
Joseph Ffrate
Robert Ffreeman
Thomas Ffreeman
Robert Ffreeman
Nicholas Ffreeman
John Ffrench
Robert Ffriend
Christopher Ffrig
Henry Ffrigg
Steephen Ffrigge
Robert Ffrith
Robert Ffrith
John Ffry
Thomas Ffryant
Mathew Ffuller
George Ffuller
Richard Ffussell
Thomas Ffyder
John G[Illegible]
John Gale
Thomas Gallon
Paule Gallophill
William Gamedge
William Gander

[Illegible] Gapper
Mathew Gardiner
Richard Gardner
Richard Gardner
Phillippe Gardner
Henry Gardner
John Garfitt
Elias Garman
William Garman
George Garnish
Robert Garraway
John Garrett
William Garrett
William Gaston
William Gattfeild
John Gaunte
Robert Gaye
James George
Richard Gibbes
John Gibbs
Alixsannder Gibbs
Robert Gibbs
John Gibson
Robt Gibsonne
Andrew Gilbert
Thomas Gilbert
Adam Gilbert
Addam Gilbert
Thomas Giles
Henry Giles
James Giles
William Giles
Henery Gilford
Richard Giller
John Ginkes
John Glade
Thomas Glannan
Edward Glover
Jeromie Glover
Peeter Goateley
Jarrad Gobbett

Robert Goberts
Hugh Godfery
Robert Godfery
William Godfery
Thomas Godman
Richard Godsland
Edward Goeringe
John Golard
William Good
Edward Goodale
Thomas Goodall
John Goodall
Richard Goodman
Thomas Goodman
Edward Goodman
Richard Goodman
Richard Goodman
William Goodridge
Nathaniell Goodwin
Thomas Goose
Richard Goreinge
William Goreinge
William Goteley
John Gouldsmith
George Grace
Walter Graunt
Rogger Gravenor
Thomas Graves
George Gray
Edward Gray
Reginald Greene
Henry Greene
Richard Greene
Peeter Greene
Edward Greene
Gyles Greene
Thomas Greene
Thomas Greeneaway
Ffrancis Greeneway
Richard Greeneway
Marke Greeneway

William Gregory
William Gregory
Thomas Gregory
John Gregory
William Greves
Ralph Grice
Thomas Griffine
Thomas Griffine
John Griffine
Thomas Griffine
George Griffine
Robert Griffine
Robert Griffine
John Griffine
Richard Griffith
Lawrence Griffith
William Grigge
William Griggson
William Grimsdale
Henry Grome
Richard Grooby
Walter Grove
Phillipe Grove
George Grymer
Robte Grymes
Edward Gubbins
William Gudderidge
William Guilford
William Guilford
Edward Gulford
Thomas Gulliner
Thomas Gulliver
John Gunstone
John Gurnett
Phillipe Guy
Phillipe Guy
John Gwyne
Nicholas Gyles
Humfery Hab[Illegible]
Richard Hackeshawe
William Hackett

William Hale
Thomas Hale
William Hall
Christopher Hall
John Hall
John Hall
Richard Hall
John Hall
Henry Hall
William Hall
John Hall
Thomas Hall
Edward Halloway
Richard Hammon
Tristeram Hammon
Richard Hammon
Richard Hammond
Richard Hanby
Robert Hancocke
Henry Hanley
Michaiell Hannan
William Hannsone
James Harden
George Hardinge
Henry Hardinge
Robert Hardinge
Richard Harford
William Harpur
William Harpur
Joseph Harris
William Harris
Edward Harris
John Harris
William Harris
Robert Harris
Thomas Harrison
Richard Harrison
Thomas Harrison
John Harrison
Christopher Harrison
Clemment Harrison

John Hart
Ambros Hart
Thomas Hart
Arthur Harte
John Harte
Michaiell Hartlye
Nicholas Hartwell
Isacke Hartwell
John Hartwell
John Harvey
Oliver Harwood
Thomas Harwood
Henry Harwood
Edward Hathaway
William Hattam
Robert Hatter
William Hatter
John Hatter
William Hatter
Richard Hatterill
Gilbert Hatterill
James Hawker
Robert Hawkes
John Hawkins
Gyles Hawkins
John Hawkins
William Haycocke
John Hayes
James Haynes
John Haynes
John Hayward
Robert Heane
John Heare
Thomas Heath
Christopher Heather
John Heather
John Heather
Hugh Heather
Thomas Heaton
Daniell Hedge
Thomas Hender

Edward Hentland
John Henwood
Miles Henwood
Robert Henwood
Michaiell Hermahan
John Herne
John Hesant
Thomas Hettystone
Thomas Hewes
Rogger Heyborne
John Heyett
Thomas Heyland
William Heyward
Robert Hiblye
Edward Hicke
William Hickley
John Hickman
John Hickman
Thomas Hicks
George Hicks
Henry Hide
Barnard Higgins
William Higglett
Xpopher Hill
John Hill
Andrew Hill
Thomas Hill
John Hill
William Hill
Anthony Hill
Humfery Hill
Mathew Hill
John Hill
George Hillar
Thomas Hilliard
Henry Hilliard
George Hilliard
William Hills
John Hills
John Hills
Anthony Hillyard

William Hingson
Richard Hipperu
Robert Hitchcocke
Thomas Hix
Phillipe Hoare
William Hobbine
Peeter Hobert
Dennis Hobsone
Robert Hockley
John Holbrooke
Nicholas Holder
Henry Holliday
Walter Holloway
Martyne Holloway
John Hollyday
Henry Holman
Ralph Holmes
William Holte
Ralph Hone
John Hone
Robert Hooke
Thomas Hooke
Robt Hooke
Henry Hooker
Marke Hooper
John Hooper
Thomas Hooper
John Hooper
Rice Hopkines
Humfrey Hopkins
Humfrey Hopkins
John Hopkins
William Hopkins
William Hopkins
George Horsley
Henry Hoskine
Humfrey Hoult
Richard Howard
Robert Howard
Phillipe Howard
Robert Howard

John Howard
Lambert Howe
John Howe
James Howe
Anthony Howell
James Howell
Rice Howell
Jeromie Howes
Thomas Howett
John Hownslowe
George Huddlestone
Richard Huddson
Peeter Hudson
Marmaduke Hudson
John Hudson
Peeter Hughes
William Humfery
Thomas Humfery
John Humferyes
John Hunt
John Hunt
William Hunt
Thomas Hunter
Ffrancis Hunter
Arthur Hunter
Thomas Hunter
Thomas Hunter
Richard Hurleburte
William Hurt
Robert Hussey
Richard Huswise
John Hutchines
Edward Hutchines
Richard Hutchines
John Hutchins
Ffrancis Hutchins
Humfery Hutchins
William Hutchinson
[Blank] Hutchinson
Ralph Hutton
Nicholas Hutton

John Hutton
John Hutton
John Hutton
Henry Hyett
Richard Hyne
Thomas Ibles
Nicholas Ingerman
Blasé Ireland
James Jackson
John Jackson
George Jackson
John James
Jerrard James
Nicholas Jane
Robert Janes
William Je[??]eris
John Jeane
Richard Jeffery
William Jelley
Edward Jellyman
Edward Jenckins
Thomas Jenckins
Thomas Jenckins
Edward Jenckins
Edward Jenckins
George Jenkins
William Jenkins
Nicholas Jenkins
John Jenkins
Edward Jenninge
William Jenninge
Peeter Jenninge
Thomas Jennings
Clement Jerome
Nicholas Jo[Illegible]
Gaberill Johnson
Thomas Johnson
William Johnson
Ralph Johnson
Thomas Johnson
Thomas Johnsone

John Jones
Edward Jones
Robert Jones
Thomas Jones
John Jones
John Jones
Robert Jones
William Jones
William Jones
William Jones
William Jones
Ffarmer Jones
Richard Jones
Beniamine Jones
John Jones
Samuell Jones
Edward Jones
Michaiell Jones
Walter Jones
George Jones
Thomas Jones
Ffrancis Jones
Thomas Jones
Edward Jones
Edward Jones
Edward Jones
William Jones
John Jones
Rice Jones
Henry Jones
Mathew Jones
Robert Jones
Thomas Jones
Charles Jones
Mathew Jones
David Jones
Rogger Jones
Ralph Jordan
Richard Jorden
William Jorden
Henry Jourye

Steepen Joyce
William Joyce
Edmond Joyce
Ffrancis Joye
William Joyner
Christopher Joyo
Edward Kathenis
Richard Keech
John Keelinge
Thomas Kellett
Richard Kelly
John Kempe
Henry Kempson
Richard Kennett
John Kennison
Edward Kent
Jeromie Kerby
Robert Kerkham
Richard Kermit
William Kettle
George Kettle
Samuell Keyes
William Kindred
William Kindred
Edward Kindred
Nathaniell Kinge
John Kinge
John Kinge
Thomas Kinge
Ralph Kinge
William Kingstone
William Kinnierlye
Thomas Kirby
James Kirkeham
John Kirkham
William Kitchell
Thomas Kitchell
Richard Kitchin
John Kitchin
Robert Kives
John Knaggstone

Thomas Knight
Ewen Knowles
William Lacy
George Lacy
John Ladler
Cuthbert Ladley
Nicholas Laine
John Lambert
John Lambert
Thomas Lamkine
Richard Lander
Thomas Lander
Edward Lane
Richard Lane
William Lane
William Lane
Edward Lane
William Langley
Robert Langley
William Langley
Anthony Langley
Peeter Langman
William Langton
Andrew Laniburie
Edward Larthe[?]
Nathan Lattimer
Thomas Launder
Peeter Lawe
John Lawrence
Hugh Lawrence
Christopher Lawrence
Rogger Lawrence
Nathaniell Layton
William Leake
Richard Ledger
Thomas Lee
John Lee
John Lee
John Lee
William Leomann
Richard Leonard

John Lettes
John Lewis
Thomas Lewis
William Lewis
Charles Lewis
William Lewis
John Lewis
George Lewis
Nicholas Lewis
Thomas Lewis
Marke Lewis
John Leyors
George Lilley
Robert Linger
Richard Linley
Jeffery Lissinnan
Richard Litler
William Loaton
Robert Locke
Lawrence Longdoor
Henry Longe
Henry Longe
John Longman
Robert Lovedale
Thomas Lovell
Thomas Lowe
Alixsannder Lowecut
Richard Lowther
Evan Loyd
Ph[Illegible] Lucas
Anthonie Lucas
William Ludlowe
George Luter
William Lylley
John Lyllye
Thomas Lyons
Richard Lywood
John Lywood
John Mabson
John Maddison
Robert Maddox

Thomas Mady
John Maggotte
John Maggotte
Richard Maggston
William Malborne
Thomas Mallard
Thomas Mamider
George Mann
Thomas Mann
Bryan Manninge
Walter Manninges
Thomas Manoringe
Thomas Manwaringe
Peeter Marbury
John Marchant
William Marchant
Ffrancis Marlow
John Marlyne
Roger Marner
William Marner
Thomas Marrett
William Marsh
Richard Marsh
William Marsh
Henry Marshall
John Marston
Robert Marston
Thomas Martyne
Robert Martyne
Thomas Martyne
John Martyne
William Martyne
Robert Martyne
George Martyne
John Martyne
Henry Mascall
Robert Masey
William Mason
William Mason
John Mason
Richard Massam

Robert Massey
Robert Masson
Anthony Mathew
Edward Mathewes
John Mathewes
Thomas Mathews
Richard Mathews
Thomas Maurice
Gyles Mawson
Gregory May
William Mayden
John Maydley
[Illegible] Mayne
Edward Meade
Jacob Meade
Ambrose Meader
Lucke Meadowes
Robert Meale
William Mealeman
Samuell Meason
John Meason
John Medlicote
Gyles Meeres
Steephen Meeres
J[Illegible] Meires
James Meredith
Ffrancis Meredith
Robert Meredith
John Merideath
Evan Merideath
Griffeth Merideth
Ffrancis Merideth
John Merideth
Morgan Merideth
John Meridith
James Merrick
Thomas Merricke
Nathaniell Merricke
John Merricke
John Merse
John Meryday

Hugh Merydieth
Edward Messenger
John Michell
John Middleton
Nicholas Middleton
Phillip Middleton
Richard Milborne
Xpopher Milborne
Rogger Miles
Robert Milford
Samuell Milton
Randolph Minshawe
Andrew Minsterley
Charles Mitchell
Steeven Mitchell
Richard Mitton
John Monday
Michaiell Moore
Andrew Moore
Andrew Moore
John Moore
John Moorecocke
Thomas Moorton
Robert Morgan
Owen Morgan
Henry Morgan
William Morgan
Lewis Morgan
Rice Morgan
Edward Morman
Thomas Morrall
Robert Morrell
Rice Morris
John Morris
Edward Morsett
Thomas Mortymer
Samuell Moss
Robert Mosse
Richard Moston
Thomas Mott
Phillipe Moyle

William Moyzes
Thomas Munday
Richard Munday
George Munday
William Muttler
Henry Myers
Robert Myles
Christopher Myres
Thomas Napkine
Edward Nash
John Nash
Robert Natt
Thomas Naylor
Richard Neathercoale
Nicholas Nelson
William Nelson
George Nelsone
John Nempas
Thomas Newell
Richard Newgood
Nathaniell Newman
Samuell Newton
William Newton
Abraham Niblett
Owin Nicholas
Edward Nicholes
Richard Nicholls
John Nightingale
Christopher Nightingale
James Norcott
Robert Norman
Thomas Norman
Edward Norris
Richard North
Beford Norton
John Nowell
William Nuttkine
Henry Nynn
James Oates
John Oates
Wilfrid Okar

Mathew Old
Henry Oran
Thomas Oren
William Oren
Peeter Orrange
John Orton
Edmound Orton
Robert Osborne
Thomas Osborne
John Ould
David Owein
Edward Owen
William Owen
George Owen
Phillipe Owen
Edward Owen
Randolph P[Illegible]
Anthony Padnall
William Page
Nicholas Painter
Symon Painter
John Pallmer
Thomas Palmer
Thomas Palmer
Ffrancis Palmer
Charells Palmer
Edward Palmer
John Palmer
John Palmer
William Parkehurst
William Parker
George Parker
John Parker
Cuthbert Parker
William Parker
Rogger Parker
Marmaduke Parker
George Parkington
Anthonie Parkinton
William Parram
Mathew Parrey

David Parrey
Edward Parry
Thomas Parry
Robert Parry
James Parry
William Parsley
Symon Parsons
William Parsons
Thomas Parsons
John Parsons
Henry Parsons
William Parsons
Adam Pashley
John Passell
William Patience
John Patteridge
Henry Paul
John Pavy
John Payne
Thomas Payne
John Paynter
Jeffery Payte
Richard Peake
Henry Peake
William Pearce
William Pearce
Abraham Peate
John Peele
William Peeris
John Peirce
John Peirce
Abraham Pelham
John Pelham
Thomas Pelsworth
Ffrancis Pengallye
Job Pennell
Thomas Penner
Thomas Pennington
John Penny
John Pennyale
Nicholas Pennyall

Nicholas Penton
Robert Pentuey
John Percy
Richard Perkins
Thomas Perkins
John Perrin
Peeter Petty
Richard Pewe
John Phetiplace
Joseph Philcocke
Phillippe Philcocke
Barnard Phillipes
Richard Phillipes
John Phillippe
William Phillippes
Ffrancis Phillipps
Thomas Phillipps
William Phillipps
John Phillips
Thomas Phillips
Ambros Phillips
David Phillips
James Phillips
Robert Phillpott
John Phillpott
John Phininier
Nicholas Pickers
Richard Pidgeon
Henry Pierce
Michaiell Piggott
John Pike
Mathew Pike
John Pinchine
John Pincombe
Ralph Pine
Abraham Plasted
John Plasted
Henry Plater
William Plater
Oliver Plater
Henry Platt

Edmond Platt
Thomas Pleasington
Bartholmew Plesington
Thomas Pollard
Robert Poole
Thomas Pooly
Rice Pope
Cornelious Pope
Richard Porte
William Porte
Robert Porthan
Edward Postine
Robert Postlett
John Postlett
Charells Potter
James Potter
Zalathiell Poulteney
William Pountner
John Powell
George Powell
John Powell
John Powell
William Powell
William Powell
Richard Powell
R[i]chard Powell
Hugh Powell
Rogger Powell
John Powell
John Powell
John Powell
Thomas Powteney
John Pratt
Mauris Predder
Thomas Preshis
John Prester
James Price
Rogger Price
Edward Price
Peeter Price
Evan Price

William Price
Grisine Price
Mathew Price
Hugh Price
John Price
Thomas Price
Evan Price
William Price
William Price
David Prichard
John Primmer
David Pritchard
Ffrancis Pritchett
Edward Procter
Thomas Prymmer
Michaiell Pryor
Henry Pulman
John Puncheon
Xpopher Purdee
John Purnell
John Purser
Richard Pursser
Edward Putny
William Puttfoote
Thomas Pynefold
John Pynefold
Nathaniell Pynefold
Henry Quinburgh
Thomas Quintal
William R[Illegible]
William Radwell
John Raineford
John Rainesterry
Richard Ramsey
John Randall
John Randall
Ralph Randall
William Randall
Cuthbert Rannicke
Symon Ransome
William Rasborowe

Edward Rawlines
Richard Rawlines
Richard Rawlines
John Rawlins
John Rawlinson
John Ray
Thomas Ray
John Raymound
Robert Read
James Reade
Cuthbert Reddhead
Robert Reddman
William Reddman
Thomas Rederife
Roger Redinge
Edward Redinge
Bonny Redman
Isacke Redman
John Reeley
Edward Rennam
William Rewell
John Reynolds
Thomas Reynolds
William Reynolds
Humfery Reynolds
Edward Reynolds
Walter Reynolds
Jacob Reynolds
David Reynolds
John Reynolds
Robert Reynolds
Edward Reynolds
William Ricards
John Rice
David Rice
Edmond Richards
Thomas Richardson
Anthonie Richardson
William Richardson
Henry Richardsone
Launcelott Richforth

William Richman
John Ridly
William Rigdon
William Riggall
William Roach
Edward Roach
Robert Roade
Mathew Roberts
Robert Roberts
William Roberts
Nicholas Roberts
Nicholas Roberts
Alixsander Robins
James Robinson
Edward Robinson
Sheffeild Robinson
James Robinson
Robert Robinson
Thomas Robinson
Robert Robinson
John Robinson
James Robinsone
Richard Robinsone
Edward Robinsone
William Robinsson
Hugh Robson
George Robson
Anthony Roche
Thomas Roe
Thomas Rogger
John Roggers
Robert Roggers
John Roggers
Hugh Roggers
Hugh Roggers
William Rolles
George Rolph
Thomas Roote
George Rootes
Symon Rootes
Richard Rowe

Rowland Rowles
Richard Rowlewright
Thomas Rowse
Thomas Rullinge
William Rummell
Edmond Russell
Henry Russell
Richard Russell
Rowland Rutlidge
John Ryder
John Rydley
Ffrancis S[Illegible]
Thomas Sachell
Michaiell Salter
James Sampson
Richard Sanders
James Sandes
William Sandway
James Sandy
William Sandy
Tobias Saule
Robert Saunders
Thomas Saunders
William Saunders
William Saunders
Nicholas Saunders
Edward Saunders
John Saunders
Joseph Savage
John Sawell
Richard Sawell
William Sawley
John Sax
Henry Saxon
Robert Say
Edward Say
Mathew Saye
John Sayer
Edward Scales
Robert Scargill
Henry Scrubbinge

Nicholas Scull
William Seabrake
Richard Seagood
George Seale
John Seamer
J[?]aniore Seares
Thomas Searson
William Seaward
George Sergant
Thomas Seward
John Sharpe
Edward Shawe
Thomas Shawe
Symonn Sheere
Thomas Sheet
Hugh Shephard
William Shepheard
Richard Shepherd
Jeoffrey Shepherd
John Shepherd
Thomas Sherwine
Thomas Shippden
Edward Shore
Ffrancis Shorter
Thomas Shotton
Thomas Shredd
Anthonie Shrowbridge
William Shugborowe
George Shugburough
John Sill
William Silvester
Edward Silvester
Richard Silvester
John Simpsone
Richard Sinettinge
Nicholas Singleton
John Skarr
Richard Skelton
Thomas Skillhorne
Richard Skynner
Richard Skynner

Edward Sleigh
George Slye
James Slye
John Smallridge
John Smart
George Smart
John Smayte
Jacob Smith
Thomas Smith
Richard Smith
Nicholas Smith
Abraham Smith
John Smith
Henry Smith
Izaacke Smith
Richard Smith
Robert Smith
Peeter Smith
John Junior Smith
William Smith
Gilbert Smith
William Smith
Robert Smith
John Smith
Robert Smith
Ralph Smith
John Smith
Rowland Smith
John Smith
Richard Smith
William Smith
John Smith
George Smith
Daniell Smith
Maurice Smith
Robert Smith
Robert Smith
Thomas Smith
James Smithes
Nicholas Smithes
Lawrence Smithy

Thomas Snape
Thomas Snape
Nicholas Snellinge
Thomas Soares
William Sower
George Sowle
Edward Spencer
David Spicer
James Spires
Gilbert Springebut
George Spure
Steephen Stagg
Richard Stagg
Richard Stagge
George Stainford
William Stainford
Richard Standish
Ceath Stanford
John Stanford
William Stanley
William Stannard
Lawrence Steed
William Steede
Richard Steeple
Thomas Steere
Walter Steevens
William Steevens
William Steevens
Anthony Steevens
George Steevens
Thomas Steevens
William Steevens
William Steevens
John Steevens
Richard Stephenson
Thomas Stephenson
John Steward
Edward Steward
Richard Stibbin
William Stich
Henry Stock

Steephen Stockdaile
John Stocke
Thomas Stocke
Thomas Stokes
Thomas Stokes
William Stone
Nicholas Stone
Robert Stoner
William Stoner
Richard Stoner
Robert Stoner
John Stoner
James Stoner
John Stoner
William Stoner
George Straine
John Strang[Illegible]
Tylbury Strange
Phillipe Strangnish
William Strangnish
Henry Strangnish
John Stridley
Richard Strowde
Hugh Struddocke
Ffrancis Stucke
John Stucke
John Studley
Thomas Styles
Thomas Styles
Ffrancis Styles
William Styles
Hercules Summers
Forename Surname
William Swaby
Miles Swaby
Richard Swan
Arthur Swan
Richard Sweete
Thomas Sy[Illegible]
Edward Sydnam
Thomas Syllers

John Symmonds
Thomas Symmonds
Richard Symmonds
John Symon
Andrew Symonds
John Symonds
Roger Symonnds
John Symonnds
Richard Symounds
Ffrancis Sympson
Thomas Sympson
John Sympson
Thomas Sympson
Henry Sympsone
William Symson
William Symson
John Tanner
John Tannor
William Tapp
Edward Tarrent
Walter Tatton
William Tayler
William Tayler
Edward Taylor
John Taylor
Jonas Taylor
John Taylor
Thomas Taylor
John Taylor
Richard Taylor
John Taylor
Marke Taylor
William Taylor
Richard Taylor
John Taylor
Thomas Taylor
William Taylor
Robert Taylor
John Taylor
John Taylor
Thomas Taylor

Thomas Taylor
William Tero
William Terrannt
John Terrey
Richard Terrey
John Terry
Thomas Terryll
Francis Terrytt
Ambrose Th[Illegible]
Abell Thomas
Symon Thomas
Morris Thomas
John Thomas
Griffine Thomas
Robert Thomsone
Henry Thomsone
Robert Thorne
John Thorpe
Thomas Thorpe
John Thorpe
George Throwbridge
Thomas Thurbury
Jacob Tinkersone
Nicholas Todd
Nicholas Todd
William Tomkins
John Tomlinson
Richard Tomlinsone
Richard Tomlinsone
Thomas Tootinge
John Townesend
Richard Townsend
Thomas Townsend
Thomas Townsend
Thomas Townsend
Peeter Towsey
Jonas Tracy
George Tradman
Lawrence Trayton
Robert Trevitt
Thomas Trike

Thomas Trisetram
Walter Tristeram
William Tristeram
Richard Troane
Thomas Trodd
William Trodd
William Trodd
Robert Trone
Peeter Trowte
Edras Trowte
William Truelove
John Trueman
Richard Tryminges
Henry Tryplett
William Tucker
John Tucker
William Tucker
William Tuckey
Thomas Tue
William Turbott
Thomas Turner
Robert Turr
Richard Tustine
William Tustone
Thomas Tyldsey
William Tyler
Nicholas Tyler
George Tyler
William Tylly
Emanuell Tylney
Nicholas Tylon
John Tyson
George Tysse
John Tyton
John Tytton
Thomas Tytton
Thomas Underwood
Tobias Urin
Ffrancis Vaughan
Robert Vaughan
Thomas Vaughan

William Vaughan
Rowland Vaughan
William Vaughan
Richard Vaughan
Richard Vaughan
Augustine Veale
Peeter Vincent
John Vincent
Thomas Waddlowe
Rowland Wade
Thomas Wadlowe
Ansell Wadmoore
John Wages
Symon Waggden
Abraham Wahan
Robert Waineman
Lawrence Walborne
William Wales
David Walker
John Wallis
Roger Walter
John Walters
Zaphan Wandall
Samuell Wanthyne
Oliver Ward
130
Thomas Ward
John Warden
John Warner
Nowell Warner
Nowell Warner
Robert Warren
John Warren
Robert Warren
Henry Warren
Thomas Warren
Thomas Warwicke
William Waters
[Illegible]h Waters
Ffrancis Waters
Ffardynando Watkin

Anthonie Watkines
Lewis Watkins
Zacharie Watkins
Lewis Watkins
Henry Watkins
John Watkins
John Watson
Richard Watson
Robt Watson
Henry Watson
Lawrence Watsone
Reynold Watterman
Marke Watters
Henry Watters
Thomas Watters
Rogger Watts
Nicholas Way[Illegible]d
Thomas Waynopp
Reynold Webb
Richard Webb
Anthony Webb
James Webb
Richard Webb
Anthonie Webb
Roger Webb
Richard Webbe
Cleament Webber
Robert Weeke
Richard Weeke
John Weeks
Symon Weight
Robert Welder
John Welsbourne
Thomas West
William West
William West
Augustus West
Thomas Westborne
Richard Westcott
John Westwood
Thomas Wexam

ohn Weyman
dward Wh[Illegible]
llen Wharfe
enry Whatley
homas Wheate
mes Wheatley
ohn Wheaton
ogger Wheaton
obert Wheeler
ogger Whippine
braham White
homas White
dward White
icholas White
obert White
ohn White
ogger White
illiam White
ohn White
ohn White
illiam White
ichard White
lixander White
hn White
seph White
bell White
chard White
chard White
hn White
ogger White
omas White
hn White
eorge White
cholas White
mond White
alter White
illiam White
rancis White
eter White
omas White
ixsander Whitehead

Thomas Whitekettle
David Whithead
John Whitingham
Thomas Whitt
John Whitterice
Richard Wickerman
Thomas Wickham
James Wiggens
John Wiggins
Thomas Wiggins
Thomas Wilbee
William Wilde
Richard Wilde
Mathew Wilde
Nicholas Wilford
Richard Wilkinson
Richard Willes
Arthur William
Rogger Williames
Augustus Williams
John Williams
John Williams
John Williams
Henry Williams
John Williams
John Williams
Rogger Williams
Thomas Williams
David Williams
Edward Williams
Evan Williams
John Williams
Thomas Williams
Richard Williams
Hugh Williams
John Williams
Jeromie Williams
John Williams
Rogger Williams
Peeter Williamson
Tomas Williamson

Addam Willis
Thomas Willis
Edmonnd Willmott
James Willoughby
Robert Wills
James Willstringe
Symon Wilson
Addam Wilson
John Wilson
Arthur Wilson
John Wilsone
John Wilsone
John Winch
Richard Winch
William Windsore
William Windsore
John Winnitt
Abraham Winns
George Winsor
Jeffrey Winter
Robert Winterton
John Winterton
Lucke Withers
John Wivell
Myles Wolmer
William Woo[Illegible]
John Wood
Michaiell Wood
Humfery Wood
John Wood
Richard Wood
John Wood
William Woodfeild
Lawrence Woodman
Henry Woodriffe
Thomas Woolridge
Leonard Wootton
Thomas Wordman
Steephen Worsley
Thomas Worthen
Thomas Worthing

Hugh Woweines
Thomas Wright
William Wright
Robert Wright
Thomas Wright
Richard Wright
Rice Wright
Thomas Wyatt
John Wyers
William Yarner
John Yearnold
Robert Yenn
Rogger Yeomans
Anthony Yonge
Robert Yonge
William Yonge
Thomas Yonge
Thomas Yonge
Ffrancis Yonge
Ffrancis Yonge
Peeter Younge
John Yoxall
Thomas [?]ssopp
William [Blank]
Lyonell [Blank]
David [Blank]
Robert [Blank]
Richard [Illegible]
Thomas [Illegible]
Thomas [Illegible]
William [Illegible]
Daniell [Illegible]
Ffrancis [Illegible]
George [Illegible]
John [Illegible]
Edward [Illegible]
Ffrancis [Illegible]
John [Illegible]
John [Illegible]
Nicholas [Illegible]
Robert [Illegible]

homas [Illegible]
/illiam [Illegible]
/illiam [Illegible]
)hn [Illegible]
ichard [Illegible]
homas [Illegible]
ichard [Illegible]
obert [Illegible]
enry [Illegible]
)hn [Illegible]
ichard [Illegible]
/illiam [Illegible]
enry [Illegible]
/illiam [Illegible]

Richard [Illegible]
Robert [Illegible]
Christopher [Illegible]
Nicholas [Illegible]
William [Illegible]
John [Illegible]
Edward [Illegible]on

Source: Public Record Office's State Papers collection, SP 16/135, piece 4.

Note: Refer to full CD version for ages, number of voyages made and rank.

Appendix XVII Transcriptions available on CD ROM

Docklands Ancestors Ltd

Archives of the Company at the Guildhall Library
1628 Admiralty Muster
1648 Petition of the Watermen for King Charles
1809 Watermen in the Navy
1899 Royal Asylum at Penge inmates and subscribers

Trueflare Ltd

Apprenticeship Bindings Indexes 1692-1908
Apprenticeship Bindings Indexes 1908-1925
Reassigned Apprentices 1688-1908
Pensioners Admitted for Relief 1794-1837
My Ancestors Worked on the Thames: A Guide to Where They Worked

All available online at www.ParishRegister.com or by post from:

Docklands Ancestors Ltd
15 Honeycroft
Loughton
Essex
IG10 3PR

INDEX

FEEDBACK

he author hopes that this guide has been of use. Comments and feedback are always
ppreciated. If you would like to contribute to the next edition of this guide or suggest
n improvement please get in touch.

ou will find much more on this subject on the author's website at
ww.ParishRegister.com. Contribution to the preservation and dissemination of our
aterman heritage is much welcomed.

mes Legon
ocklands Ancestors Ltd
5 Honeycroft
oughton
ssex
10 3PR

ww.ParishRegister.com